D044200b

F14028

CLASSIC

LATERAL
THINKING
CHALLENGES

CLASSIC

LATERAL
THINKING
CHALLENGES

By Paul Sloane and Des MacHale

Illustrated by Myron Miller

Main Street
A division of Sterling Publishing Co., Inc.
New York

Library of Congress Cataloging-in-Publication Data Available

10   9   8   7   6   5   4   3   2   1

Published by Sterling Publishing Co., Inc.
387 Park Avenue South, New York, NY 10016
© 2005 by Sterling Publishing Co., Inc.

Material in this collection adapted from:
Intriguing Lateral Thinking Puzzles © 1996 by Paul Sloane and Des MacHale
Improve Your Lateral Thinking © 1998 by Paul Sloane and Des MacHale
Ingenious Lateral Thinking Puzzles © 1998 by Paul Sloane and Des MacHale

Distributed in Canada by Sterling Publishing
℅ Canadian Manda Group, 165 Dufferin Street
Toronto, Ontario, Canada M6K 3H6
Distributed in Great Britain by Chrysalis Books Group PLC
The Chrysalis Building, Bramley Road, London W10 6SP, England
Distributed in Australia by Capricorn Link (Australia) Pty. Ltd.
P.O. Box 704, Windsor, NSW 2756, Australia

Printed in China
All rights reserved

Sterling ISBN 1-4027-2361-X

CLASSIC
LATERAL THINKING
CHALLENGES

CONTENTS

INTRODUCTION

Lateral thinking puzzles are often strange situations which require an explanation. They are solved through a dialogue between the quizmaster, who sets the puzzle, and the solver or solvers, who try to figure out the answer. The puzzles, as presented, generally do not contain sufficient information for the solver to uncover the solution. So a key part of the process is the asking of questions. The questions can receive one of only three possible answers—yes, no, or irrelevant.

When one line of inquiry reaches an end, then another approach is needed, often from a completely new direction. This is where the lateral thinking comes in.

Some people find it frustrating that, for any puzzle, it is possible to construct various answers that fit the initial statement of the puzzle. However, for a good lateral thinking puzzle, the proper answer will be the "best"—in the sense of the most apt and satisfying. In real-life too, most problems have more than one possible solution. A good lateral thinker will not accept the first solution found but will continue to look for new and creative approaches.

These problems teach you to check your assumptions about any situation. You need to be open-minded, flexible and creative in your questioning, and able to put lots of different clues and pieces of information together. Once you reach a viable solution you keep going in order to refine it or to replace it with a better solution. This is lateral thinking!

PUZZLES

WARM-UP PUZZLES

ANGRY RESPONSE

A man called his wife from the office to say that he would be home at around eight o'clock. He got in at two minutes past eight. His wife was extremely angry at his late arrival. Why?

Clues: 151/Solution: 223.

PICTURE PURCHASE

An art expert went to a sale and bought a picture he knew to be worthless. Why?

Clues: 192/Solution: 258.

ALONE IN A BOAT

Why are two little animals alone in a little boat in the middle of the ocean?

Clues: 151/Solution: 223.

STRANGULATION

A famous dancer was found strangled. The police did not suspect murder. Why not?

Clues: 206/Solution: 271.

COMPLETE GARBAGE

The garbage was emptied out of the cans and a man died. How?

Clues: 162/Solution: 233.

GOLF BAG

During a golf competition, Paul's ball ended up in a bunker inside a little brown paper bag that had blown onto the course. He was told that he must either play the ball in the bag or take the ball out of the bag and incur a one stroke penalty. What did he do?

Clues: 174/Solution: 243.

FLIPPING PAGES

Yesterday, I went through a book, which I had already read, in a peculiar manner. After I finished a page, I flipped to the next page, then rotated the book 180 degrees. After that page, I rotated the book 180 degrees and then flipped to the next page, rotated the book 180 degrees again, and continued in this fashion until I was done with the whole book. What was going on?

Clues: 172/Solution: 240.

LEADFOOT AND GUMSHOE

A woman is stopped for speeding. The police officer gives her a warning, but the woman insists that she be given a ticket and a fine, which she promptly pays. Why did she want the ticket and fine?

Clues: 181/Solution: 249.

MAN IN TIGHTS

A man wearing tights is lying unconscious in a field. Next to him is a rock. What happened?

Clues: 182/Solution: 250.

STRAIGHT AHEAD

When the Eisenhower Interstate Highway System was built, it was specified that one mile in every five must be absolutely straight. Why?

Clues: 206/Solution: 271.

MOTION NOT PASSED

A referendum motion was not passed. If more people had voted against it, however, it would have passed. How come?

Clues: 185/Solution: 252.

RUSSIAN RACER

At the height of the Cold War, a U.S. racing car easily beat a Russian car in a two-car race. How did the Russian newspapers truthfully report this in order to make it look as though the Russian car had outdone the American car?

Clues: 198/Solution: 264.

WATERLESS RIVERS

Now for a riddle: What has rivers but no water, cities but no buildings, and forests but no trees?

Clues: 216/Solution: 279.

THE TEST

The teacher gave Ben and Jerry a written test. Ben read the test, then folded his arms and answered none of the questions. Jerry carefully wrote out good answers to the questions. When the time was up, Ben handed in a blank sheet of paper while Jerry handed in his work. The teacher gave Ben an A and Jerry a C. Why?

Clues: 209/Solution: 274.

FIRED FOR JOINING MENSA

Mensa is a club for clever people. Anne's employer has no anti-Mensa feeling, but has made it clear to her that if she ever joins Mensa she will lose her job. How come?

Clues: 171/Solution: 240.

SIX-FOOT DROP

A man standing on solid concrete dropped a tomato six feet, but it did not break or bruise. How come?

Clues: 202/Solution: 267.

STATUE OF AN INSECT

Why is there a commemorative statue of an insect in a little town in the state of Alabama?

Clues: 205/Solution: 269.

SEVEN BELLS

A little shop in New York is called The Seven Bells, yet it has eight bells hanging outside. Why?

Clues: 200/Solution: 266.

REENTRY

What took nineteen years to get into itself?

Clues: 196/Solution: 262.

ASSAULT AND BATTERY

John is guilty of no crime, but he is surrounded by professional people, one of whom hits him until he cries. Why?

Clues: 152/Solution: 224.

UP IN THE AIR

One hundred feet up in the air, it lies with its back on the ground. What is it?

Clues: 215/Solution: 279.

CLEAN SHAVEN

Why did Alexander the Great order all his men to shave?

Clues: 161/Solution: 232.

ADOLF HITLER

During the war, a British soldier had Adolf Hitler clearly in the sights of his gun. Why didn't he fire?

Clues: 150/Solution: 222.

WINNING NUMBERS

I have on a piece of paper the winning numbers in next week's lotto jackpot. I am an avid gambler, yet I feel I have very little chance of winning. Why?

Clues: 218/Solution: 281.

FAIR FIGHT

A boxer left the ring after winning the world championship. His trainer took all the money and he never got a cent. Why not?

Clues: 169/Solution: 239.

UNKNOWN RECOGNITION

I saw a man I had never seen before, but I immediately knew who he was. He was not famous and had never been described to me. He was not unusual nor doing anything unusual. How did I recognize him?

Clues: 214/Solution: 278.

RIDDLE OF THE SPHINX

The Sphinx asked this famous riddle: What is it that goes on four legs in the morning, two legs in the afternoon, and three legs in the evening?

Clues: 197/Solution: 263.

UNCLIMBED

Why has no one climbed the largest known extinct volcano?

Clues: 213/Solution: 277.

TALKING TO HERSELF

A woman is talking sadly. Nobody can understand her, but a man is filming her intently. Why?

Clues: 208/Solution: 273.

EASY PUZZLES

MAN OVERBOARD

A man vacationing abroad was alone on his yacht when he fell off into deep water. He was a nonswimmer and was not wearing anything to help keep him afloat. He was rescued half an hour later. Why didn't he drown?

Clue: 183/Solution: 250.

HIGH BLOOD PRESSURE

During a medical examination, Gerald's blood pressure is found to be three times that of a normal healthy person. Yet neither Gerald nor his doctor is particularly worried about this. Why?

Clue: 177/Solution: 245.

THE GREAT WALL

An American, who had never been to any country other than the United States, was standing one day on solid ground when he saw the Great Wall of China with his own eyes. How come?

Clue: 175/Solution: 244.

RECOVERY

A truck driver called in to his office to report that his truck had broken down. A tow truck was sent out to tow back the disabled truck. When they arrived, the truck that had broken down was towing the tow truck. Why?

Clue: 196/Solution: 262.

POOR DELIVERY

A Denver company ordered some goods from a European supplier. The American firm was very precise in stating the dates on which it wanted the deliveries to occur.

However, the European company, which generally had a high reputation for dependability, missed every delivery date by at least one month. Some shipments were very early and others were very late. Why?

Clue: 193/Solution: 259.

THE PILOT'S SON

A man and his son were traveling on a scheduled flight across the Atlantic. The man asked the flight attendant if his son could have a look inside the cockpit. The boy was allowed to do this and the pilot gladly explained about the plane and its controls. After the boy left, the pilot turned to the copilot and said to him, "That was my son." How could that be?

Clue: 192/Solution: 258.

HOLE IN ONE

A golfer had dreamed all her life of hitting her tee shot straight into the hole. However, one day she did this and was not at all pleased. Why not?

Clue: 177/Solution: 245.

CIRCULAR TOUR

It has often been observed that individuals lost in a desert will set off with the intention of walking in a straight line but will eventually return to their starting point. Why is this?

Clue: 161/Solution: 232.

A RIDDLE

An old riddle goes like this:

A man without eyes, saw plums on a tree.
He did not take plums and he did not leave plums.
How could this be?

Clue: 197/Solution: 263.

A DOOR TOO LARGE

A man bought a door to fit in a door frame. The door was too large, so he cut off a piece. He found it was too small. So he cut off another piece. This time the door fitted perfectly. How come? (He cut pieces only off the door, he did not cut the frame.)

Clue: 167/Solution: 237.

RADIO BROADCAST

One summer a Polish radio station, in an attempt to render a service to listeners, broadcasted a noise which was proven to deter mosquitoes while not bothering humans. The station received a barrage of complaints from listeners. Why?

Clue: 195/Solution: 261.

HIDE-AND-SEEK

The children had been playing hide-and-seek for some time when Jackie said, "I can't play anymore. It is obvious that anyone could find me now." "It depends who is doing the seeking," said Joan. "Most of us would find you easily, but for John it would be just as hard to find you as anyone else who was hiding." She was right. What was going on?

Clue: 176/Solution: 245.

DANCE BAN

A bar in Rio has a regular dance competition every Thursday night. It banned one man from entering because he kept winning. He was not a professional dancer or schooled in dancing. Why did he keep winning?

Clue: 164/Solution: 235.

THE MISSING MONEY

A man went to a cash-dispensing machine outside a New York bank and withdrew $200, which he carefully put into the back pocket of his trousers. He spent $30 that day. The next day, when he reached into the back pocket of his trousers, he found only $5. Nobody had robbed him. What had happened?

Clue: 185/Solution: 252.

500 TIMES

Florence has 500 times as many as Washington. Of what?

Clue: 171/Solution: 240.

BOUNCING BABY

How could a baby fall out of a twenty-story building and live?

Clue: 156/Solution: 227.

THE TOWER

A man went to the top of a 180-foot-high cylindrical tower. He leapt off, but was uninjured. Why?

Clue: 210/Solution: 275.

THE SLOW-CAR RACE

A special endurance test involved two drivers and their cars. They were told to drive one hundred miles out into the desert, rest for no more than one hour, and then drive back. The catch was that the last car back would be the winner.

The two drove out very slowly. During the rest period, one of the drivers began to doze. The other driver immediately drove back as fast as he could. Why did he do this?

Clue: 202/Solution: 267.

THE DRIVE

A man and woman in a car drove down the drive from their house to the road. The man was behind the wheel. When they reached the road they got out and changed places. The woman turned the car around, then they swapped places again and the man drove back down the drive to the house. They did this several times. Why?

Clue: 168/Solution: 237.

HOMECOMING

An executive who was based in New York was posted to Hong Kong on an assignment. When he was due to return, he faxed his manager the following request: "Is it OK for me to transport back to New York, at the company's expense, my personal items, household effects, and junk?" He was given approval and did so.

A furious argument ensued. The company refused to pay the transportation charge and, in the end, the executive had to sue the company. He won, but that is not the issue. The question is: What was the cause of the argument?

Clue: 177/Solution: 246.

BYPASS

The people of a small French town were very annoyed by the traffic, especially the heavy trucks, that travelled the one main road running through the town. To eliminate the problem, they built a modern bypass road that was much wider than the road through the town. However, they soon found that they got at least as many trucks going through the town as before. Why?

Clue: 158/Solution: 229.

ELEMENTARY PUZZLES

BOSTONIAN

A man was born in Boston, Massachusetts. Both his parents were born in Boston, Massachusetts. He lived all his life in Boston but he was not a United States citizen. How come?

Clues: 155/Solution: 226.

THE TREE AND THE AXE

A woman bought a young tree and put it in her garden. The next day she took an axe to it. Why?

Clues: 211/Solution: 275.

BELOW PAR

A middle-aged man took up golf for the first time and within a month he went around his local course in under 90 shots. However, he was not pleased. Why?

Clue: 154/Solution: 225.

SCHOOL FRIEND

Joe went back to his hometown and met an old school friend he had not seen for years. His friend said, "I am married now but not to anyone you know. This is my daughter."

Joe turned to the little girl and asked her her name. She said, "I have the same name as my mother."

"Then you must be called Louise," said Joe. He was right, but how did he know?

Clues: 199/Solution: 264.

SELL MORE BEER

A management consultant went into a bar one evening. After a little while he told the bar owner a simple and quite legal way of selling a lot more beer. However, the bar owner was not pleased. Why not?

Clues: 200/Solution: 265.

THE CLINCH

A prim lady was disgusted that the teenage boy and girl in front of her at the cinema remained locked in a passionate embrace throughout the entire feature. She called the manager, who immediately summoned an ambulance. Why?

Clue: 162/Solution: 232.

PRECOGNITION

A lady knocked at the door of a tiny cottage and when an old lady opened the door she said, "Good morning, Mrs. Turner." Neither of them had ever met, or seen or heard of the other before. How did she know the old lady's name?

Clue: 194/Solution: 260.

DUD CAR

The Chevrolet Nova was a successful car in many countries, but not in Mexico. Why not?

Clues: 168/Solution: 237.

THE LUMBERJACKS

Tim and Joe are two lumberjacks who work at the same rate of speed. One morning, Tim works steadily from 8 o'clock to noon without taking a break. Joe starts and finishes at the same times, but he takes a five-minute break every half-hour. At the end of the period Joe has felled considerably more trees than Tim. How come?

Clue: 182/Solution: 249.

RED LIGHT

A police officer was sitting on his motorcycle at a red traffic light when two teenagers in a sports car drove by him at 50 miles per hour. He did not chase them or try to apprehend them. Why not?

Clues: 196/Solution: 262.

NUN-PLUSSED

A priest sitting in a doctor's waiting room was horrified to see a crying nun, rushing from the doctor's office, followed by a flustered doctor. Angrily he asked the doctor for an explanation. What explanation did the doctor give?

Clue: 188/Solution: 255.

CONFECTIONERY MANUFACTURER

A manufacturer of confectionery has a work force of thousands of workers. They never strike or demand better conditions. They work up to twenty hours per day and receive no wages except food and shelter. Yet every year a completely new work force is brought in and none of the existing workers is re-employed. Why?

Clues: 163/Solution: 233.

THE PAINTER

Much of his painting was seen at the city's two large art galleries but no one had ever heard of him. Why not?

Clues: 190/Solution: 257.

REGULAR ARGUMENTS

Every evening a man and a woman would eat at a table and then have a violent argument, swearing, shouting and insulting each other. The rest of the time they got on very well, with never a cross word. Why did they argue every night?

Clues: 197/Solution: 263.

BEAUTIFUL GIRLS

As a group of sailors emerged from their ship after months at sea, one spindly wimp bet his fellow sailors that he would have a beautiful girl on each arm within an hour. How did he win his bet?

Clue: 154/Solution: 225.

ORANGE TRICK

There is an orange in the middle of a circular table. Without touching or moving the orange or the table, how could you place a second orange under the first?

Clue: 190/Solution: 256.

THE BOOKMARK

A man who needs a bookmark is offered a fine bookmark for a dollar. Why does he refuse it?

Clue: 155/Solution: 226.

THE FALL

A man fell 140 feet (43m) without a parachute. He turned upside down seven times and came to land safely on solid ground. How come?

Clues: 170/Solution: 239.

A HAIRY STORY

A man who was completely bald met a doctor at a party. She had lovely short black hair. He explained that he had tried hair restorers and transplants but without any success. She sympathized. "If you could make my hair look like yours, I would gladly pay you $1000," he said.

"O.K., I'll do it," she answered. How did she win the $1000?

Clues: 175/Solution: 244.

GOOD-BYE, MOTHER

A young woman in a restaurant was approached by a tearful old lady who said, "You look so like my own daughter who passed away last year. Could you do me a favor and say 'Good-bye, Mother' when I leave?"

The young woman happily agreed and said, "Good-bye, Mother" when the old lady left. Later she got a shock. What was it?

Clue: 174/Solution: 243.

STEER CLEAR OF THE BANKS

A man drove into town and parked at the end of the main street. He got out of his car and went up to the bookstore at the opposite end of the street. He then came back down the street to his car and drove off. There are three banks on the main street, but the man did not walk past any of them. Why not?

Clue: 205/Solution: 270.

BY THE RIVER

A police officer saw a man standing by a river holding a loaded gun near his head. The officer rushed towards the man and grabbed the gun. A minute later he handed the gun back with apologies. Why?

Clues: 158/Solution: 229.

INTRIGUING PUZZLES

THE HELICOPTER

A helicopter was hovering 200 feet above the sea when the pilot suddenly turned off the engine. The rotor stopped but the helicopter did not crash. Why not?

Clues: 176/Solution: 245.

CAR IN THE RIVER

A man was driving alone in his car when he spun off the road at high speed. He crashed through a fence and bounced down a steep ravine before the car plunged into a fast-flowing river. As the car slowly settled in the river, the man realized that his arm was broken and that he could not release his seat belt and get out of the car. The car sank to the bottom of the river. He was trapped in the car. Rescuers arrived two hours later, yet they found him alive. How come?

Clues: 159/Solution: 230.

CALL BOX

A lady depended on a public telephone booth to make calls but it was frequently out of order. Each day she reported the problem to the telephone company but nothing was done. Finally she phoned the company with a false piece of information, which caused the telephone to be fixed within hours. What did she tell them?

Clues: 159/Solution: 229.

TWO JUGS

A man had a jug full of lemonade and a jug full of milk. He poured them both into one large vat, yet he kept the lemonade separate from the milk. How?

Clues: 212/Solution: 277.

SPEEDING TICKET

A man is driving his car at ten miles an hour down a quiet suburban street when a police officer spots him and fines him for speeding. Why?

Clues: 204/Solution: 269.

TWIN TROUBLE

Bob and Sam were identical twins born in London in 1911. Bob was born before Sam but Sam was older than Bob. How come?

Clues: 212/Solution: 276.

THE TYPIST

A young woman applied for a job as a secretary and typist. There were dozens of applicants. The woman could type only eleven words per minute, yet she got the job. Why?

Clues: 213/Solution: 277.

LIBRARY LUNACY

A public library suddenly announced that each member could borrow up to ten books and not return them for up to six months. Why?

Clues: 181/Solution: 249.

FALL OF THE WALL

In its day, the Great Wall of China was considered virtually impregnable, yet it was breached within a few years of being built. How?

Clues: 170/Solution: 239.

ELEVATOR

A woman was in an elevator. She was frightened. She sat down. She laughed and stood up. Why?

Clues: 168/Solution: 238.

SMART APPEARANCE

Victor was smartly dressed, well shaven, and with the best haircut he had had for years. Many of his friends and relatives saw him, yet no one complimented him. Why not?

Clues: 203/Solution: 268.

DOGS HOME

A boy brings home a lost puppy but his parents order him to dispose of it. As he walks into town, wondering what to do, he sees a truck with DOGS HOME printed on it. He slips the puppy into the truck, but this leads to a minor disaster. Why?

Clues: 167/Solution: 237.

TITLE ROLE

A vain actress was thrilled to hear from her agent that she had received the title role in the movie of a famous book. But later she was very displeased. Why?

Clues: 210/Solution: 275.

JOB LOT

A builder was very pleased to buy a job lot of bricks at a very low price. When he examined them he found that they were sound, strong and well made, but he was extremely unhappy. Why?

Clues: 180/Solution: 248.

INVALUABLE

A man got something of little value. It became very valuable so he threw it away. If it had been worth less, he would have kept it. Why?

Clues: 179/Solution: 247.

THE CRASH

In heavy fog, there was a serious car accident which involved two trucks and six cars. All the vehicles were severely damaged. Police and ambulances were quickly on the scene, where they found both truck drivers and took them to the hospital for treatment. However, no drivers from any of the cars could be found at the scene of the accident. Why not?

Clues: 163/Solution: 234.

THE LIFEBOAT

A man was cast adrift in a lifeboat. He was horrified to see that it was letting in water, so he diligently bailed out the water. After two days, he did not bother bailing out the water anymore. Why not?

Clues: 182/Solution: 249.

WESTWARD HO!

(West) Bristol —— Reading —— London (East)

Two men set off on foot one morning. They started from Reading and headed east towards London. They walked until they reached a restaurant where they sat down and had lunch. They then carried on walking east towards London. They arrived that same afternoon in Bristol. Since the only direction in which they walked was east, how was it possible for them to arrive in Bristol?

Clues: 217/Solution: 280.

40 FEET AHEAD

A man set out for a walk. At the end of his walk his head had travelled 40 feet farther than his feet had travelled. He was a healthy man with all his limbs intact before and after the walk. So how did his head travel farther than his feet?

Clues: 172/Solution: 241.

THE CIRCULAR TABLE

A lady has an expensive circular oak table and she wishes to find its exact center. How does she do this without marking the table in any way?

Clues: 161/Solution: 232.

T-SHIRTS

A change in the law in Italy resulted in large sales of white T-shirts with black bands on them. How come?

Clues: 208/Solution: 273.

TWO SUITCASES

A man is carrying two suitcases, one in each hand. One is a big empty suitcase. The other is a smaller light suitcase full of books. He puts the smaller suitcase into the bigger one, making it heavy and difficult to carry. Why does he do this?

Clues: 213/Solution: 277.

THE NONCHALANT POLICE OFFICER

One fine morning, a police officer was walking down the high street in the middle of town. Turning a corner, he gasped as he saw two armed robbers dash out of a bank, firing guns as they left. He then ignored them, and continued on walking up the street. Why?

Clues: 187/Solution: 254.

CHALLENGING PUZZLES

RARE EVENT

What happened in the second half of the 20th century and will not happen again for over 4000 years?

Clues: 196/Solution: 262.

HOLY ORDERS

A priest goes into a church carrying a loaded gun. Why?
(P.S. He was not a canon!)

Clues: 177/Solution: 245.

WELL DRESSED

Why did an old lady always answer the door wearing her hat and coat?

Clues: 216/Solution: 280.

KID STUFF

Many more children are involved as pedestrians in road accidents than might be expected from their numbers and road use. An expert on road accidents has put forward an ingenious theory to account for this. What do you think the theory might be?

Clues: 180/Solution: 248.

THE TWO DRIVERS

Two drivers drove slowly and safely in the correct direction down a wide road before coming to a stop in front of a red stop light. A nearby police officer immediately arrested one of the drivers and let the other one drive off. The police officer had never seen or heard of either driver before. Neither driver had a criminal record. They were both fully dressed and no one had been drinking. Both cars were in excellent roadworthy condition and had not been stolen. The arrested driver was charged and convicted. Of what?

Clues: 212/Solution: 276.

HOW TO CHOOSE A BUILDER

A man wanted to construct an important building and he received offers from a hundred builders, who each presented their qualifications and claimed to be the best builder around. How did he eventually choose between them?

Clues: 178/Solution: 246.

KEYS IN THE CAR

A man locks his keys inside his car and is unable to get them out despite trying for an hour. A police officer comes along and offers to help. He discovers that the back door of the car is unlocked and he consequently recovers the keys. The man thanks him, but when the officer departs the man locks the back door, leaving the keys inside. Why?

Clues: 180/Solution: 248.

THE HASTY ROBBER

A man robbed a bank. If he had seen the other gun he would not have been in such a hurry. Why not?

Clues: 176/Solution: 244.

THE UNLUCKY GAMBLER

A very unlucky gambler had lost all his money. His friends organized a raffle, rigged so that he would be sure to win. Knowing the ticket number he held, they filled a hat with tickets bearing the same number. They then had him draw the winning number. "Well," they asked him, "who won?"

"Not me, anyway," he replied sadly. What had happened?

Clue: 214/Solution: 278.

THE CODE

The doorman at an exclusive club says one word to each prospective entrant. If the entrant answers correctly he is allowed to enter; otherwise, he is rejected.

A hopeful nonmember observed carefully as a member approached. The doorman said, "Twelve." The member replied, "Six." He was admitted. A second member came up. The doorman said, "Six." The member replied, "Three." He was admitted. The man now decided that this was easy and he stepped forward. The doorman said, "Ten." The man replied, "Five." The doorman angrily kicked him out. What should he have said?

Clues: 162/Solution: 233.

BRUSH-OFF

Amanda was doing something important when she received a phone call from Zoe, who was long-winded and boring. How did Amanda quickly finish the call without offending Zoe?

Clues: 156/Solution: 227.

TIME OF ARRIVAL

A teenage boy returned home from a party very late and silently crept upstairs to his bedroom. No one saw or heard him arrive. Next morning when his mother asked him what time he had arrived home, he replied, "About one o'clock." How did she know that he had, in fact, arrived much later?

Clues: 210/Solution: 275.

A SOLUTION OF PAINT

A problem which had caused the loss of many thousands of lives and the loss of millions of dollars worth of property was solved with a can of paint and a brush. What was the problem?

Clue: 203/Solution: 268.

STRIKING THE ELEPHANT

A man uses a stick to strike a part of an elephant and after a few seconds it disappears. The man is then a lot richer. Why?

Clues: 206/Solution: 272.

DEPRESSURIZATION

A pilot was flying alone at an altitude of 30,186 feet when he heard a rattling noise in the plane. He immediately depressurized the plane, i.e., let the air out and allowed the pressure in the plane to drop to that of the outside atmosphere. A sudden depressurization is generally considered very dangerous, so why did he do this?

Clues: 166/Solution: 236.

MUTILATION

Why did a man deliberately douse himself with sulfuric acid?

Clues: 186/Solution: 253.

STRANGE REACTIONS

John and Joan, who both enjoyed their work, were given surprises one morning. John was told that he was being laid off that week because there was no further work for him. Joan was told that she was being promoted and would get a pay raise. Joan cried for the rest of the day, while John laughed. Why?

Clues: 206/Solution: 271.

THE ARCHAEOLOGIST

A professor of archaeology was on an excavation at a site when he found an ancient and interesting item. He took it home and put it in his study. His wife and children were away so there was no other person in the house. He locked up and went to bed. In the morning, he was horrified to find the item gone. A thorough search showed it was not in the house. There had been no break-in and no one else had entered or left the house. What had happened?

Clues: 152/Solution: 224.

DESERT

A man walked alone for days across a desert. He did not take water or any kind of drink with him. He did not find water. How did he survive?

Clues: 166/Solution: 236.

THE DEADLY DIAMONDS

A Bedouin prince had three diamonds which he kept in a box with a sliding lid that he kept firmly closed. The box also contained two deadly cobras which would attack any stranger foolish enough to open the box. One day a thief sneaked into the prince's tent and within moments had safely stolen the diamonds. How did he do it?

Clues: 166/Solution: 236.

GAZE AWAY

A man walked into a room full of normal people. None of them would look him in the eye. Why not?

Clues: 173/Solution: 242.

THE CONTAINER

King Arthur gave one of the knights of the Round Table a bottomless metal container in which for many years he kept flesh and blood. What was it?

Clue: 163/Solution: 233.

WORKOUT PUZZLES

THE UNLUCKY BED

A certain bed in a certain hospital acquires the reputation of being unlucky. Whichever patient is assigned to this bed seems to die there on a Friday evening. A watch is kept by camera and the reason is discovered. What is it?

Clues: 214/Solution: 278.

MISSING ITEMS

What two items does a boy have at ten years of age that he did not have when he was one year old?

Clues: 184/Solution: 252.

ONCE TOO OFTEN

If you do it once, it's good. If you do it twice on the same day, though, it's a serious crime. What is it?

Clues: 189/Solution: 256.

REJECTED SHOES

A man bought a pair of shoes that were in good condition and that fit him well. He liked the style and they looked good. However, after he had worn them for one day he took them back to the shop and asked for a refund. Why?

Clues: 197/Solution: 263.

NOTEWORTHY

A woman took a picture of a U.S. president to her bank. As a result a criminal was arrested. How?

Clues: 188/Solution: 255.

SLOW DRIVE

Why does a man drive his car on a long journey at a steady fifteen miles per hour? The speed limit is well above that and his car is in full working order and capable of high speeds.

Clues: 202/Solution: 267.

WEAK CASE

The police charged a man with a crime. They had a weak case against him. He posted his bail. The police then had a strong case against him. Why?

Clues: 216/Solution: 280.

THE MAN WHO GOT WATER

A man parked his car on the road, walked into a building, returned with some water, and poured the water onto the sidewalk. Why?

Clues: 183/Solution: 250.

THE WRITER

A man who was paralyzed in his arms, legs, and mouth, and unable to speak a word, wrote a best-selling book. How?

Clues: 219/Solution: 282.

CHIMNEY PROBLEM

An industrial archaeologist was examining an abandoned factory in a remote place with no one in sight or within earshot. He climbed to the top of an old 100-foot chimney by means of a rusty old ladder attached to the outside of the chimney. When he got to the top, the ladder fell away, leaving him stranded. How did he get down?

Clues: 161/Solution: 231.

HAPPY BIRTHDAY

A man went into his local shopping center. A woman whom he had never met before wished him a happy birthday. How did she know it was his birthday?

Clues: 175/Solution: 244.

ACIDIC ACTION

A murderer killed his wife and dissolved her body completely in a bath of acid. What piece of evidence caused him to be caught?

Clues: 150/Solution: 222.

NOVEMBER 11

A large mail order company performed an analysis of its customers. It was surprised to learn that an unusually large number were born on November 11. How could this be?

Clues: 188/Solution: 255.

GARBAGE NOSINESS

One morning last week I peered into my neighbor's garbage can and then drove to work feeling annoyed. One morning this week I peered into my other neighbor's garbage can and then drove off feeling even more annoyed. Why?

Clues: 173/Solution: 242.

SHOOTING A DEAD MAN

A policeman shot a dead man. He was not acting illegally. Why did he do it?

Clues: 201/Solution: 266.

WELL-MEANING

How did an animal rights activist who had good intentions cause the death of the living creatures she was trying to save?

Clues: 217/Solution: 280.

BOTTLED UP

A cleaning woman asked the man she worked for if she could take home his empty bottles. When she got home, she threw them out. Why did she do this?

Clues: 156/Solution: 226.

ALEX FERGUSON

In the early 1990s, Alex Ferguson was the coach of Manchester United, the most successful professional soccer team in England at that time. Previously he had been a very successful manager in Scotland. He would be a very successful manager of a soccer team anywhere in the world, except Singapore. Why is that?

Clues: 151/Solution: 223.

DON'T GET UP

A woman is reading a newspaper alone. She hears the phone ring in the room next to the one she is in. Although she knows that the call is probably important, she does not bother to answer it. Why not?

Clues: 167/Solution: 237.

SCUBA DO

Why was a man driving down the street wearing a scuba face mask?

Clues: 199/Solution: 265.

MISUNDERSTOOD

Part of the police manual gives instructions in a language that none of the policemen speaks. Why?

Clues: 185/Solution: 252.

DIFFICULT PUZZLES

EXPORT DRIVE

During the 1930s, how did some Japanese businessmen overcome American mistrust of goods made in Japan?

Clues: 169/Solution: 239.

BOMBS AWAY

A bomber plane, which was in perfect working order, was over its target. The tea that the pilot had been drinking sat in its cup at his elbow. The plane released its bombs, but they did not fall from the plane. Why not?

Clues: 155/Solution: 226.

SPACE SHUTTLE

Why is it that a plane is allowed to take off and fly in a thunderstorm, but the space shuttle is not?

Clues: 203/Solution: 268.

SMALL FURNITURE

A factory specializes in producing furniture that is twenty percent smaller than normal furniture. The furniture is not designed for or sold especially to smaller-sized people. Why do they make it?

Clues: 202/Solution: 268.

SUSPENSE

A man traveling by train awoke to find his railcar suspended twenty feet in the air. Why?

Clues: 207/Solution: 272.

THE WOMAN IN THE DITCH

A beautiful woman walked across a field several times. She deliberately walked in a six-inch ditch. Why?

Clues: 218/Solution: 281.

GREASE

A man covered the head of a stranger in grease. Why?

Clues: 175/Solution: 244.

CASH IN HAND

Smith had owed Jones a thousand dollars and, although Jones asked for the sum many times, Smith never paid it back. Then one day Smith offered to repay Jones the thousand dollars in cash, but Jones refused to accept it. Why?

Clues: 160/Solution: 230.

ANYWHERE IN THE WORLD

A pilot was due to fly his plane from one place to another when a man asked if he could be given a lift. The pilot said, "Yes, for a small fee that is possible. I can drop you off on my way." "But you don't know where I am going," replied the man. "Surely that makes a big difference." "Not at all," said the pilot. How could this be so?

Clues: 152/Solution: 223.

THE NOSY STUDENT

Judy, a young woman studying at college, was unfortunate to have a roommate who was rude, lazy, selfish, and inquisitive. Judy was annoyed because, while she was at lectures, her roommate would look through Judy's desk and read Judy's personal mail. How did Judy overcome this problem?

Clues: 188/Solution: 255.

POOR EQUIPMENT

A man took an expensive piece of equipment with him on a journey. When he reached his destination he found that the equipment, though in perfect working order, was of practically no use. Why not?

Clues: 193/Solution: 259.

STAND AT THE BACK

During a flight from Brazil to London, the pilot told all the passengers to get out of their seats and to stand at the back of the plane. Why did he do this?

Clues: 204/Solution: 269.

THE STATUE

A huge and very heavy statue had to be lifted onto a large pedestal base in the middle of a town square. The bottom of the statue was completely flat and there was no way of lifting it except by putting ropes around and under it. How did they manage to get the ropes out from under the statue once it was lifted onto the base?

Clues: 205/Solution: 269.

POLICE VISIT

Before you can buy a car in Tokyo, the police must first come and visit you. Why?

Clues: 193/Solution: 259.

LARGE AND SMALL

Why, on the same day, were several groups of strong, fit, large people taking instructions from puny, small people?

Clues: 181/Solution: 248.

PENTAGON PANIC

One day during the cold war, a young officer rushed into his superior's office in the United States Department of Defense in Washington, D.C. "We have discovered," he said, "that if both we and the Russians launch our missiles at exactly the same time, their missiles would hit the United States before our missiles hit Russia." "Are our missiles slower?" asked his superior. "No, they have exactly the same power, weight, and speed." "Is the distance they fly shorter?" "No, both distances flown are exactly the same." "Well, what is the reason?" Can you tell?

Clues: 191/Solution: 257.

PAGE 78

Every week a woman went into the local library. If she saw a book that looked interesting, she immediately turned to page 78 before deciding whether she should borrow the book or not. Why?

Clues: 190/Solution: 256.

THE BOOK

A man walked into a bookshop and bought a book even though he could not understand a word of the language in which the entire book was written. Why did he buy it?

Clues: 155/Solution: 226.

THE SERVICE

A man regularly used and paid for a particular service that was provided by a large organization. The organization announced that, as a special promotion, it would offer all customers the service for one week at one-tenth of the normal price. The man refused this offer and continued to pay the normal price during the special promotion week. Why did he do this?

Clues: 200/Solution: 265.

STRENUOUS PUZZLES

THE UNBROKEN ARM

Why did a perfectly healthy young girl put a full plaster cast on her arm when it was not injured in any way?

Clues: 213/Solution: 277.

EXCEPTIONAL GRATITUDE

Why did Bill thank Ted for some eggs that Bill had never received and that Ted had never given?

Clues: 169/Solution: 238.

DALI'S BROTHER

Some time after Salvador Dali's death, his younger brother became famous as (believe it or not) a surrealist painter. This younger brother had great international success and the word "genius" was used to describe him. His name was Dali and he did not change it. Yet today, the world remembers only one Dali and few people even know that he had a brother. Why is this?

Clues: 164/Solution: 234.

ONE MILE

If you go to your atlas and look at the western edge of the state of South Dakota where it borders Montana, you will see a straight line with a kink of about one mile. Everywhere else the border is a straight line. The kink does not benefit any local landowner and no other states are involved. Why is the kink there?

Clues: 189/Solution: 256.

THE SHOPLIFTER

A shoplifter starts stealing small items and over a period of time steals larger and larger items, but then suddenly stops altogether. What is going on?

Clues: 201/Solution: 267.

GETTING AWAY WITH MURDER

A man shot his wife dead. She was not threatening him or anyone else. He then gave himself up to the police. They released him. Why?

Clues: 174/Solution: 242.

BARE BONES

During an examination, a medical student is handed a human femur (thigh bone). The examiner asks the student, "How many of these do you have?"

The student replies, "Five."

"Wrong," says the examiner, "You have two femurs."

But the student was right. How come?

Clues: 153/Solution: 225.

THE POWER OF TOURISM

In a certain place the local authorities, in order to increase tourism, have made the price of electricity higher. Why?

Clues: 194/Solution: 260.

WIPED OUT

A woman got a job with a large company. After her first day's work she returned home utterly exhausted because of a misunderstanding. What had happened?

Clues: 218/Solution: 281.

88 TOO BIG

A man died because his number was 88 too big. How come?

Clues: 168/Solution: 237.

THE AUCTION

A man went to an auction to bid for something he wanted. He expected to pay about $100 for it, but ended up paying $500. There was no minimum price and no one bid against him. What happened?

Clues: 153/Solution: 224.

INVISIBLE

What can you stand in front of in broad daylight and not see, even if you have perfect eyesight?

Clues: 179/Solution: 247.

POOR INVESTMENT

Why did a company spend millions of dollars trying to find something that costs only a few thousand dollars?

Clues: 194/Solution: 260.

NONEXISTENT ACTORS

Why did the credits of a well-known movie list the names of four nonexistent actors?

Clues: 188/Solution: 254.

MACHINE FORGE

A man builds a machine into which he feeds colored paper. Out of the other side come perfect $100 bills. Experts cannot tell them from real ones. How does he do it and why does he sell the machine?

Clues: 182/Solution: 250.

TWO CLOCKS

A man was given two clocks by his wife as a Christmas present. He did not collect clocks and they already had plenty of clocks in the house. However, he was very pleased to receive them. Why?

Clues: 212/Solution: 276.

SPRAYING THE GRASS

The groundskeeper at a sports complex watered the grass every evening when the sun was setting. The grass grew fine. Before a major event, though, he sprayed the grass during the midday heat. Why?

Clues: 204/Solution: 269.

WONDER HORSE

A horse that had lost every one of its previous races was entered in a horse race and came in first ahead of a top-class field. No drugs were used, and if the jockey had not confessed, then nobody would have known. What happened?

Clues: 218/Solution: 282.

ADRIFT IN THE OCEAN

Two men are in a boat drifting in the Atlantic Ocean a hundred miles from the nearest land. They have no drinking water onboard, no radio, and they have no contact with any other boats or people. Yet they survive for a long time. How?

Clues: 150/Solution: 222.

NO MORE BORE

A notorious bore once called on Winston Churchill, who sent his butler to the door to say that Churchill was not at home. What suggestion did Churchill make to the butler to convince the caller that he really was not at home?

Clues: 187/Solution: 254.

PROMOTION

John is a young man working for a big company. He is lazy, poorly motivated, and inefficient. Yet he is the first person in his department to be promoted. Why?

Clues: 195/Solution: 261.

BARREN PATCH

A farmer has a patch of ground in the middle of one of his most fertile fields on which nothing will grow. Why not?

Clues: 154/Solution: 225.

JOB DESCRIPTION

Two men were sitting in a crowded restaurant. A woman who was a total stranger to both of them walked in and told them her job. She said nothing more and they said nothing. What was going on?

Clues: 180/Solution: 248.

SHAKING A FIST

A policeman stopped a man for dangerous driving. As the policeman walked toward the car, the man rolled down the window and waved his fist at the policeman. Later, he thanked the policeman for saving his life. Why?

Clues: 200/Solution: 266.

THE WRONG BALL

A golfer drove his ball out of sight over a hill. When he got there, he saw a ball that was the same make as his own and identical to it in every way. But he knew immediately that it was not his ball. How come?

Clues: 219/Solution: 282.

BURNT WOOD

Over the past 100 years many men have dedicated significant portions of their lives to the quest for some burnt wood. Although they have sometimes been successful, the burnt wood has never moved. What is it?

Clues: 157/Solution: 228.

WINDOW PAIN

A builder builds a house that has a square window. It is two feet high and two feet wide. It is not covered by anything. The person for whom the house is being built decides that the window does not give enough light. He tells the builder to change the window so that it gives twice the amount of light. It must be in the same wall, and it must be a square window that is two feet high and two feet wide. How does the builder accomplish this task?

Clues: 217/Solution: 281.

GAS ATTACK

A man was sentenced to ten years' imprisonment with hard labor because he had kept the gas mask that the army had issued him. Why?

Clues: 173/Solution: 242.

SUPER-STRENUOUS PUZZLES

FINGERPRINT EVIDENCE

The mass murderer Ted Bundy was very careful never to leave any fingerprints at the scene of any of his crimes, and he never did. Yet fingerprint evidence helped to incriminate him. How come?

Clues: 171/Solution: 240.

PENTAGON PUZZLE

The headquarters of the U.S. defense operations is the Pentagon in Arlington, Virginia. Why does it have twice as many bathrooms as it needs?

Clues: 191/Solution: 258.

DEBUGGING

How were insects once used in the diagnosis of a serious disease?

Clues: 166/Solution: 236.

BALD FACTS

A woman fell in love and, as a result, lost all her hair. Why?

Clues: 153/Solution: 225.

FILL HER UP!

A woman bought her husband a beautiful new sports car as a present. When he first saw it, he filled it with wet cement and completely ruined it. Why?

Clues: 171/Solution: 240.

HOSING DOWN

Because it was raining, the firemen hosed down the road. Why?

Clues: 178/Solution: 246.

REPLACING THE LEAVES

During fall, a little girl was in her backyard trying to stick the fallen leaves back onto the trees with glue. Why?

Clues: 197/Solution: 263.

THREE SPIRALS

A woman was pleased when she received three spirals instead of the usual two. When it was discovered that she had received three spirals, she was arrested. Why?

Clues: 210/Solution: 274.

YOU CAN'T BE TOO CAREFUL

Millions of people buy a particular medicine. The disease for which the medicine is effective is one that these people have virtually no chance of catching. What do they buy?

Clues: 219/Solution: 282.

NONCONVENTIONAL

In a convent, the novice nuns at the dinner table are not allowed to ask for anything such as the salt from the other end of the table. This is because they should be so aware of one another's needs that they should not need to ask. How do they get around this prohibition?

Clues: 187/Solution: 254.

THE RANSOM NOTE

A kidnapper sent a ransom note. He prepared it carefully and ensured that it contained no fingerprints. Yet it was used to prove his guilt. How?

Clues: 196/Solution: 262.

BIOGRAPHY

An author died because he wrote a biography. How did he die?

Clues: 154/Solution: 225.

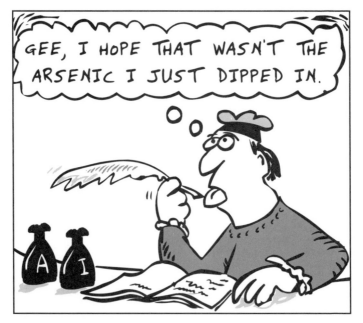

FREE LUNCH

A man in a restaurant used two forks and one knife. He did not pay for his lunch. What was happening?

Clues: 173/Solution: 241.

CARTOON CHARACTER

What cartoon character owes his existence to a misprint in a scientific journal?

Clues: 160/Solution: 230.

SECRET ASSIGNMENT

The famous physicist Ulam one day noticed that several of his best graduate students had disappeared from his university. They had in fact gone to Los Alamos to take part in the top-secret preparations for the first atomic bomb. They were sworn to secrecy. How did Ulam find out where they had gone?

Clues: 199/Solution: 265.

ANCIENT ANTICS

We generally consider ourselves to be a lot smarter and better educated than the people who lived in the prehistoric periods of the Stone Age, Iron Age, and Bronze Age. But what was it that men and women did in those times that no man or woman has managed to achieve for the last 4,000 years?

Clues: 151/Solution: 223.

THE CARPET SELLER

I bought a beautiful plain carpet measuring nine feet by sixteen feet from the carpet seller. When I got home I realized that my room was actually twelve feet by twelve feet. I returned to the carpet seller, who assured me that I could now exactly fit my room, provided I made just one cut to the original piece. Can you figure out how to do it?

Clues: 159/Solution: 230.

NO RESPONSE

A man often answered questions in the course of his work. One day a stranger asked him a perfectly reasonable question that he refused to answer. Why?

Clues: 187/Solution: 254.

WALKING BACKWARD

A man walked backward from the front door of his house to his kitchen. Someone rang the doorbell and the man ran quickly out of his back door. Why?

Clues: 216/Solution: 279.

RIGHT OFF

A man comes out of his house to find that his new car is damaged beyond repair after he has paid for it, but before he has had time to insure it. However, he is absolutely delighted at what has happened. Why?

Clues: 198/Solution: 263.

PASS PROTECTION

In the city where I live, commuters on the mass transit system can use monthly passes or single tokens. Today, I saw long lines of commuters waiting to buy passes and tokens. Those people with passes or tokens were able to bypass the lines. However, even though I had neither a pass nor a token, I was also able to walk right up to the turnstiles and pass through. How come?

Clues: 191/Solution: 257.

BUSINESS RIVALRY

Cain and Abel are business rivals. Cain cuts his price, and Abel then undercuts him. Cain then cuts his price even lower than Abel. Abel slashes his price to a ridiculous level and gets all the business, forcing Cain out of the market. But Cain has the last laugh. Why?

Clues: 158/Solution: 229.

FULL REFUND

A young couple went to a theater to watch a movie. After fifteen minutes they decided to leave. They had had a perfectly good view of the movie, which was running in perfect order. The cashier gave them a full refund. Why?

Clues: 173/Solution: 241.

A DAY AT THE RACES

A man was returning from a day at the races where he had made a lot of money. He was speeding in his car and was stopped by the police. The policeman took down all his details, but the man was never prosecuted nor suffered any penalty. Why not?

Clues: 165/Solution: 235.

PEOPLE PUZZLES

THE POSTMAN

A postman had to deliver a letter to a house that was surrounded by a five-foot wall. The house could be approached only by the main path. Unfortunately, a ferocious dog was tied by a long lead to a tree nearby, so that the path was well within the dog's range. If the postman walked up the path, he was sure to be attacked by the dog. How did he outmaneuver the dog and deliver the letter?

Clue: 194/Solution: 260.

THE PROFESSORS

Two professors of mathematics glared at each other as they examined the same elementary equation. It had been written by a ten-year-old child. "This equation is correct," said one. "No, it is absolutely wrong," said the other. How could two experts disagree so completely about a simple equation?

Clues: 195/Solution: 261.

THE RUNNER

When a runner reached the end of a long, gruelling marathon, officials were amazed to see him continue to run. Why did he do this?

Clue: 198/Solution: 264.

THE BOSS

One day a boss said to his employees, "I can fight and beat any man who works here." A new employee, a seven-foot-tall ex-prizefighter, stood up to take on the boss. What did the boss do?

Clue: 155/Solution: 226.

THE STOCKBROKER

Why did a stockbroker continue to send out to many people forecasts of stock price movements that he knew would be wrong?

Clue: 205/Solution: 270.

THE VENTRILOQUIST

It was only when he died that the secret of a great ventriloquist was discovered. What was it?

Clue: 215/Solution: 279.

THE GOLFER

Jones was playing in a golf match that he very much wanted to win. He was on the green and using his putter. He carefully lined up his putt, aimed at the hole, and then deliberately putted the ball right over and beyond the hole. Why did he do this?

Clues: 174/Solution: 243.

THE QUATORZIÈME

In Paris, a man with a job known as a *quatorzième* sits in his place of work in the evening. Sometimes he is called on to do something, but most evenings he is not. What does he do?

Clues: 195/Solution: 261.

THE CARTOONIST

Why does the United States Air Force employ the services of a top-class cartoonist?

Clues: 160/Solution: 230.

THE SWIMMER

In 1967, Sylvia Ester, an East German Olympic swimmer, swam the one hundred-meter freestyle in a time of 57.9 seconds, a new world record. But this was never recognized or acknowledged. Why not?

Clues: 208/Solution: 273.

THE MILLIONAIRE

A man working late at the office left some sandwiches on his desk. As a result of this, he later became a multimillionaire. How?

Clues: 184/Solution: 251.

THE CLIMBER

A climber bought an expensive new pair of climbing boots. On his first outing with them he found that they were too tight, so he changed into some old boots he had brought. He did not want to carry the new boots all the way up the mountain and back, but he feared that if he left them behind they would be found and kept by another climber. What did he do?

Clues: 162/Solution: 232.

THE SALESMAN

A door-to-door salesman visited a house in order to demonstrate an excellent new model of vacuum cleaner. As part of the demonstration, he emptied a small bag of soot on a carpet. To his embarrassment the vacuum cleaner would not pick up the soot. Why not?

Clues: 199/Solution: 264.

THE FARMER

A greedy and miserly farmer worked hard and tended his crops very carefully. Suddenly, he dashed out one day and dug up a field that had a crop of half-grown hay. It was a little wet, but there was nothing wrong with the crop. He subsequently had to resow the field, and the whole episode cost him much time and money. Why did he do it?

Clues: 170/Solution: 239.

THE SECRETARY

A secretary went on vacation. She inadvertently took with her something from the office. Her boss sent her a message asking her to return it immediately. This she did. Yet, when she returned from vacation, she was dismissed. Why?

Clues: 199/Solution: 265.

THE ENGINEER

An engineer was studying a dam when he was suddenly killed. How?

Clues: 169/Solution: 238.

THE INVESTIGATOR

A private investigator followed a man. He waited until the man parked his car and went off. The investigator then let the air out of one of the tires on the man's car. Waiting at a distance, he watched as the man returned, examined the flat tire, and then walked off. The investigator then went home, pleased with his day's work. What had he been hired to do?

Clues: 179/Solution: 247.

CRIME PUZZLES

GREAT DETECTION

A masked robber passed a note to a bank teller. It said, "I've got a gun. Hand over all the money in your till." The teller did so and the robber made good his escape. Within twenty-four hours, the police had arrested him. What mistake had he made?

Clue: 175/Solution: 244.

HEADLINE NEWS

A jury found John Jones guilty of murder, and the judge passed the death penalty on him. The judge then returned to his chambers, sat down for a cup of coffee, and picked up a copy of the afternoon paper. The headline read, "John Jones Guilty— Sentenced to Death." The judge was baffled that the paper could have printed the story in so short a time. How could they?

Clue: 176/Solution: 244.

ROBBERY

A gang of criminals was loading a van with television sets that they were stealing from a warehouse when they suddenly heard the siren of an approaching police car. They could not avoid or outpace the police car. How did they escape?

Clue: 198/Solution: 264.

THE BAD DRIVER

James was a notoriously bad driver. He always drove much faster than the speed limit, through red traffic lights, and up one-way streets the wrong way. He was known to the police as the worst and most dangerous driver in town. Yet, for twenty years, he did not have any kind of traffic accident, was not arrested or cautioned by the police, and kept a clean license. How come?

Clue: 153/Solution: 225.

POINT-BLANK SHOT

A man walked up to a naked woman, pointed a gun at her heart, and shot her. She survived. How?

Clues: 192/Solution: 258.

THE TRIAL

A man was on trial for the murder of another man, despite the fact that the body had not been found. During the trial there was a sensational announcement that the man who had been murdered was, in fact, alive and in the next five seconds was about to enter the courtroom. The murdered man, however, did not arrive, and the prosecutor then claimed he could prove the defendant guilty. How?

Clues: 211/Solution: 275.

THE FORGER

A forger spent years studying the U.S. $100 bill until he produced what he felt was a perfect forgery. However, he was arrested the first time he tried to pass one. Why?

Clue: 172/Solution: 240.

POISONED

An old man was poisoned. The police found that he had eaten and drunk nothing on the day of his death. How had the poison been administered?

Clues: 193/Solution: 258.

THE GOLDEN VASE

A very valuable golden vase was in the middle of a large room in a museum. It was surrounded by an electronic field that formed a complete sphere around the vase. If anything pierced the electronic field, the alarm bells would ring and guards appear in seconds. An enterprising thief worked out a way to break into the museum, but he knew that, if he set off the alarm, the guards would arrive before he could escape with the vase. How did he steal the vase and escape without being caught?

Clues: 174/Solution: 243.

THE UNHAPPY PATIENT

A man suffering from pains was examined by a doctor who correctly diagnosed the condition. The doctor did nothing. The pain went away. The man was unhappy. Why?

Clues: 214/Solution: 278.

THE UNSUCCESSFUL ROBBERY

A gang of armed robbers burst into a large bank. They demanded all the money from the tills. The bank manager pointed out that there was none. They then insisted that he open the safe. He did so but there was no money inside. Just then the police arrived and arrested the gang. What was going on?

Clues: 214/Solution: 278.

THE BURGLARY

A couple went on holiday, leaving their house empty but well secured. They had left their keys with a very careful and honest neighbor. When they returned, they found that they had been robbed of many valuables including jewelry, video equipment, etc. There was no sign of any break-in. How had it happened?

Clues: 157/Solution: 227.

MURDER

An elderly woman is found dead in her bed. She has been murdered. In her bedroom is a fine collection of plates. The police established that she was in good health, seemed perfectly fine when she went shopping the day before, and that no one else had recently visited or entered the house. How did she die?

Clues: 186/Solution: 252.

A SHOOTING

At a party two men, Rob and Bill, became engaged in a violent quarrel. Rob pulled a gun and, in plain view of many witnesses, shot Bill dead. The police were called. They questioned Rob and the witnesses. They decided that it was a case of murder, yet they pressed no charge against Rob. Why not?

Clues: 201/Solution: 266.

ANOTHER SHOOTING

A police officer shot a woman dead. Someone else was charged with her murder and found guilty. How come?

Clues: 152/Solution: 223.

SPEEDING

A man who was driving well in excess of the speed limit was chased by a police car for several miles. Then the man saw another police car in front of him on the road so he pulled over. The officers from both cars came over to him. They had both clearly seen him speeding, yet neither arrested him nor gave him a ticket. They simply gave him a warning and let him go. Why?

Clues: 204/Solution: 268.

HISTORICAL PUZZLES

JAM DOUGHNUT

Why did a famous statesman and world leader stand up in front of a large group of people and say, very seriously, "I am a jam doughnut"?

Clue: 180/Solution: 247.

WITHOUT DROUGHT

How did the American Civil War lead to a reduction in droughts in various parts of the world?

Clue: 218/Solution: 281.

CROSS THE GORGE

It was decided to build a suspension bridge over a deep and wide gorge. The river at the bottom of the gorge was too violent for any boat to cross. How did the engineers get the heavy cables from one side of the gorge to the other?

Clues: 164/Solution: 234.

THE END OF THE WAR

How do we know that the war between Lydia and Media in Asia Minor ended on precisely May 28, 585 B.C., in our dating system?

Clue: 168/Solution: 238.

THE STIFF GATE

Several people were invited to dinner in a private house. They found that it was quite difficult to open the front gate as it was very stiff. At dinner, one of the guests commented on this and the host smiled. He then explained why he had made the gate hard to open. What was the explanation?

Clues: 205/Solution: 270.

THE TWELVE

From the beginning of time and up to the time of this writing, twelve and only twelve people have achieved this feat. What is it?

Clues: 211/Solution: 276.

THE FORGERY

A historical researcher was presented with a document purported to be an authentic mid-eighteenth-century bill signed by the King of England. How did he know at once that it was a forgery?

Clues: 172/Solution: 241.

ACROSS THE RIVER

In the early days of exploration in America, a group of explorers came to a deep, wide river. There was no bridge, and they had no boats or material to make boats. They could not swim. How did they get across?

Clues: 150/Solution: 222.

THE IMPOSTOR

A woman once came forward and claimed to be Anastasia, heiress to the Russian throne. How did the authorities quickly discover that she was an impostor?

Clues: 179/Solution: 247.

BRUNELLESCHI'S CHALLENGE

Filippo Brunelleschi is one of the great figures of the Italian Renaissance; he was a sculptor, goldsmith, and architect. His greatest masterpiece is the dome of the cathedral in Florence, which he completed in 1417. He had to win the commission for the dome against stiff competition. The story is told that he won by issuing a challenge to his competitors to stand an egg upright on a flat table without using any other materials. No one else could do it. How did Brunelleschi do it?

Clues: 156/Solution: 227.

HOUDINI'S CHALLENGE

The great conjurer and escapologist Harry Houdini was an expert with locks and safes. He was once challenged by a safe manufacturer to open a locked safe. Before accepting the challenge, Houdini examined the safe carefully and saw that it was of a new design that he would almost certainly find impossible to unlock. Nevertheless, he accepted the challenge, and won it. How?

Clues: 178/Solution: 246.

THE BUILDING

A man was very relieved one day to reach a building and go inside. It was a place he normally disliked. There was no one there to meet him, and there was nothing for him to do there. Why was he so pleased?

Clues: 157/Solution: 227.

MOTIONLESS

A young man combed his hair and then sat in a chair for twenty minutes without moving a muscle. Why did he do this?

Clues: 185/Solution: 252.

HOMING SPANIARDS

During the early days of their conquests of Central and South America, Spanish soldiers often had to travel long distances through strange, uncharted country. Sometimes they travelled at night. They developed an excellent method of ensuring that they could always find their way back to their base. How?

Clues: 177/Solution: 246.

THE COURTIER

King Alfonso XIII of Spain (1886–1931) apparently employed a man at court with just one specific function in relation to music. What was that function?

Clues: 163/Solution: 233.

GRUESOME PUZZLES

AGELESS

A young couple were separated shortly after they met and they did not come face to face again for fifty years. By that time he had become an old man, but she had not aged at all. In fact, she looked exactly as he had seen her fifty years before. Why?

Clue: 151/Solution: 222.

THE ROCK

A man, going about his business, brushed against a rock. Within minutes he was dead. Why?

Clue: 198/Solution: 264.

THE BREEZE

A man was standing up on a bright sunny day, happy to feel the breeze in his face. He knew that if the wind dropped he would die. Why?

Clue: 156/Solution: 227.

THE ACCIDENT

A careless driver caused an accident. Fortunately, both he and the driver of the other car were wearing seat belts and were uninjured. However, a passenger in the other car (who was not wearing a seat belt) was very badly mangled in the accident and lost both his legs as a result. When the case came to court the careless driver escaped with a small fine. Why was the judge so lenient?

Clue: 150/Solution: 222.

THE NONCHALANT WIFE

A woman came home one evening and switched on the light in her living room. She was horrified to see the remains of her husband lying on the floor. He had committed suicide. Ignoring the situation, the woman had a cup of coffee and went calmly about her housework, and did not phone for medical assistance or the police. Why not?

Clues: 187/Solution: 254.

TWO MEN

A man died a nasty death and another man many miles away was at last happy even though they had never met and no grudges were borne. What was going on?

Clues: 213/Solution: 277.

A MYSTERIOUS DEATH

A healthy man went out for a walk one evening and was later found dead. The police examined the body carefully but were mystified as to the cause of death. No one else was involved. A postmortem revealed that the man had been killed by a freak accident that left virtually no trace. What was it?

Clues: 186/Solution: 253.

THE CRUEL KING

Two men were asked by their king to carry out a certain task. They did this entirely to his satisfaction and went to him seeking their just reward. However, the king decreed instead that they both be severely punished. Why did he do this?

Clues: 164/Solution: 234.

THE DEADLY CLIMB

A group of healthy men walked up a mountain. One of them died. If the man who died had climbed the mountain on any other day, he would have lived. What happened?

Clues: 165/Solution: 235.

TOO POLITE

Japanese office workers strive to be very polite. One was killed because he was too polite. How?

Clues: 210/Solution: 275.

DEAD MAN, DEAD DOG

A man and his dog were found dead in the middle of a field. The man was wearing wading boots. No one else was around. How had they died?

Clues: 165/Solution: 235.

AXE ATTACK

A woman knocked on a stranger's door and asked to use the bathroom. She came out and killed the man with an axe. Why?

Clues: 153/Solution: 224.

THE MAN WHO SHOT HIMSELF

A man who was alone in a room very carefully and deliberately pulled out a gun and shot himself. Some time later, another man was charged with his murder and found guilty. What happened?

Clues: 183/Solution: 250.

FIENDISH PUZZLES

LIGHT SAVING

In the subway of a major American city, the stealing of light bulbs was a common occurrence and a major problem. The sockets for the light bulbs were within easy reach and could not be moved. How did the city authorities solve this problem and practically eliminate the theft of light bulbs?

Clues: 182/Solution: 249.

MATCHLESS

A particular person born in January 1978 has a unique distinction. What is it?

Clues: 184/Solution: 251.

AN ODD NUMBER

What is peculiar about the number 8549176320?

Clues: 189/Solution: 255.

THE LESS-COSTLY CAPITAL

One of the world's capital cities spends much less (both as a proportion of its budget and in absolute terms) than other capital cities on a social service which is generally considered vital. Why is this?

Clues: 181/Solution: 249.

STOP/GO

A group of responsible people, not pranksters, drive around a city in their car. When they stop for a traffic light, they do not go, even if the light has turned green, until a car behind them toots its horn. Why do they do this?

Clues: 206/Solution: 271.

VANISHING POINT

A man paid a great deal of money to travel to an exotic location, but when he returned he found that he had never really been there at all. Why? Where was it?

Clues: 215/Solution: 279.

BUS STOP I

A man is standing at a bus stop carrying an ordinary kitchen chair in his hands. Why?

Clues: 157/Solution: 228.

BUS STOP II

A woman travels by bus to a certain building every day. There are two bus stops on her side of the street. One is one hundred yards before the building and the other is 200 yards beyond the building. She always gets off at the bus stop two hundred yards past the building and walks back. Why?

Clues: 158/Solution: 228.

STRINGING ALONG

A man carefully glued tiny pieces of glass to a length of string. At first he was very pleased with the results. But later he regretted doing it. Why?

Clues: 207/Solution: 272.

ONE INCH SHORTER

A man went to work one day and by the end of his day's work he was one inch shorter. Why?

Clues: 189/Solution: 256.

THE SIGNAL

John stood in an enclosed room watched by three men. The room had no windows or openings, but solid walls, floor, ceiling, and door. There was no telephone or electrical device of any kind. The three men (who all had good eyesight and hearing) watched John carefully in silence. They observed no change in condition, sound, or movement. Yet, while they were watching, John signalled to his partner, James, in a nearby room and passed a message to him. How?

Clues: 202/Solution: 267.

WESTERN SUNRISE

As we all know, the sun rises every day in the east and sets in the west. One day, a man saw the sun rise in the west. How?

Clues: 217/Solution: 280.

TEENAGE PARTY

While his parents were away, a teenage boy and his friends drank some of the parents' gin. This was of course strictly forbidden. They then poured water into the gin bottle to return the level to where it had originally been, and put the bottle back exactly where they had found it. However, when the couple came home, the father took one look at the bottle of gin and turned angrily to his son to denounce him for illicit drinking. How had he known?

Clues: 209/Solution: 274.

COWARDLY ACT

Why did a coward deliberately expose himself to significant danger?

Clues: 163/Solution: 233.

FALL OF THE HALL

A well-designed and structurally sound building owned by the government suddenly collapsed. Why did this happen?

Clues: 170/Solution: 239.

THE CICADA

There is one kind of cicada (an insect sometimes known as a cricket) which has a 17-year life cycle. It lives dormant, underground, for 16 years as a grub, then emerges for one year as an active insect. What possible survival advantage can such a 17-year life cycle have?

Clue: 161/Solution: 231.

SWEET IN POCKET

Because he had a sweet in his pocket, a man invented something which is found in most modern kitchens. What is it?

Clues: 207/Solution: 272.

MICKEY MOUSE'S GIRLFRIEND

Why were a group of grown men running around asking each other who was Mickey Mouse's girlfriend?

Clues: 184/Solution: 251.

THE PAINTING

A painter gave his aunt an ugly abstract painting which she stored in the attic. However, when he came to stay she hurriedly hung it on the wall of her parlor, but unfortunately she hung it upside down. What did she say when he pointed this out?

Clues: 190/Solution: 257.

THE PARCEL

Why did a lady deliberately leave a parcel behind her on a bus?

Clues: 190/Solution: 257.

THE SUITCASE AND THE BOX

A man came out of a large building carrying a suitcase and box. He was very happy. He went into a smaller building and a few minutes later emerged from the smaller building very angry and carrying just the suitcase. What was going on?

Clues: 207/Solution: 272.

THIRD PLACE

A man enters a competition confidently expecting to win, but he only comes in third. However, he is very amused. Why?

Clues: 209/Solution: 274.

THE MISSING DIAMOND

A man kept a precious diamond in a safe. Nobody else knew the combination. It was not written down. Nobody ever saw him open the safe. Yet one day when he opened the safe, the diamond was gone. How come?

Clues: 184/Solution: 251.

PADDLE YOUR OWN CANOE

A man set out to paddle his canoe down a slowly flowing river from one point to another. He found that no matter how quickly he paddled, it made no difference to the time it took for his journey. Why not?

Clues: 190/Solution: 256.

POOR IMPERSONATION

An actress is hired to impersonate an heiress who has died. The actress looks very much like the heiress. Her acting is superb. She watches videos of the woman and works tirelessly in front of a mirror to develop an excellent imitation of the woman's appearance, mannerisms and voice. Yet she is soon exposed as an impostor. Why?

Clues: 194/Solution: 260.

CREEPY CRAWLIES

A man moves into a new house and finds that his garden is crawling with insects, slugs, snails, caterpillars, and unwanted bugs. He goes to his local cinema, community hall and bars (where he knows nobody) and asks for a donation to help clear his garden. Everyone responds very generously and he is able to solve his problem. What happened?

Clues: 163/Solution: 234.

CATCHING A BULLET

A man fires a bullet from a gun and another man catches the bullet with his bare hands. The bullet does not touch anything (except air, of course) from the gun to the hand. The second man is uninjured. How does he do it? (There are two good solutions to this problem. Can you find them both?)

Clues: 160/Answers: 231.

DOCTOR'S APPOINTMENT

A woman has an appointment to visit the doctor. When she gets there the receptionist tells her that there is a new doctor and that he cannot see the woman just yet as he is on the telephone. The woman waits and then the doctor calls her in and says that he is sorry he kept her waiting but he had some important telephone calls to handle. Within moments the doctor is highly embarrassed. Why?

Clues: 167/Solution: 236.

SWEET WHEAT

A farmer wins first prize for his wheat every year in an agricultural show in stiff competition with his neighboring farmers. However, after the show is over, he sends each of his fellow competitors a bag of his best wheat seed. Why?

Clues: 208/Solution: 273.

THREE NOTES

One morning a woman wrote the same note to three different people. The first was a bank robber, who laughed at the note and threw it away. The second was a Bolivian, who also threw the note away. The third was a priest, who was very sad to receive the note. What was happening?

Clues: 209/Solution: 274.

DEADLY PUZZLES

THE DEADLY MELODY

A woman heard a tune which she recognized. She took a gun and shot a stranger. Why?

Clues: 166/Solution: 236.

THE SIGN

A man and his wife were in their car. The man saw a sign. Without either of them saying a word, he drew a gun and shot his wife dead. Why?

Clues: 201/Solution: 267.

NEW SHOES

A woman bought a new pair of shoes and then went to work. She died. Why?

Clues: 186/Solution: 253.

THE ARCHDUKE

When Archduke Ferdinand was shot, in 1914, his attendants could not undo his coat to stem his bleeding wound. Why not?

Clues: 152/Solution: 224.

THE HASTY PACKER

She died because she packed too quickly. How did she die?

Clues: 176/Solution: 244.

HEARTLESS

A man who was surrounded by other people suddenly had a heart attack. Everyone saw this but no one intervened. He subsequently died. There was no ill-will towards him, and no physical barrier between him and the others. Why did no one try to help him?

Clue: 176/Solution: 245.

DEAD DRUNK

A man was coming home after a night out drinking. There was no one around, so he decided to relieve himself. Within minutes he was dead. What happened?

Clues: 165/Solution: 235.

THE BIG ROOM

A man is lying dead in a big room. Musical instruments lie around. He is holding a bottle of brandy. He died because of the brandy, but how?

Clues: 154/Solution: 225.

SACRIFICE

Three castaways were starving on a desert island. When they had run out of food they decided that one of them had to die to be eaten by the other two. All three were single, of the same age, experience, size and skills. But they easily decided who should die. How?

Clues: 198/Solution: 264.

STOLEN FINGER

A man sneaked into a morgue one night and cut the little finger off a corpse. Why?

Clues: 205/Solution: 271.

POOR DOGS

During WWII, why did German soldiers have to shoot the dogs they had carefully trained?

Clues: 193/Solution: 259.

AFTER-SHAVE

A man is given a bottle of after-shave for his birthday. He puts some on and later that day he dies. How?

Clues: 151/Solution: 222.

RADIO DEATH

A man is driving his car. He turns on the radio and hears music. He stops and shoots himself. Why?

Clues: 195/Solution: 261.

UNTYING THE ROPES

When they untied the ropes, everyone knew he was dead. How?

Clues: 215/Solution: 278.

CAPSIZE

A riverboat in good condition is steaming down a calm river when it suddenly capsizes, drowning most of the passengers. What happened?

Clues: 159/Solution: 229.

MURDER IN THE NEWSPAPER

An old man read a report in his morning newspaper about a wealthy woman who had died of old age. "She was murdered!" he gasped. Then he carried on reading the rest of the newspaper. How did he know that it was murder and why did he do nothing about it?

Clues: 186/Solution: 253.

THE MAN WHO RETURNED TOO SOON

One bright sunny morning a man left his home. After some time he decided to return home and came back straightaway. When he got home he died. If he had not gone home so quickly he would have lived. What happened?

Clues: 183/Solution: 250.

THE PERFECT MURDER

Edward carefully plotted the murder of his wife. One winter's day he strangled her in the bedroom, then faked a burglary. He ransacked the house, scattered possessions and broke through the patio doors. He set the burglar alarm downstairs before driving to the local golf course to establish his alibi. Two hours later, when

Edward was in the middle of his golf game with three colleagues, the burglar alarm went off and the police were alerted. They found the house apparently broken into and the wife strangled. No animals or electrical devices were found which could have set the alarm off, so it looked as though an intruder had set off the alarm before killing the poor woman. Edward was never arrested or charged. The police inspector long suspected Edward, but there was one question which he could not fathom: How did the suspect get the burglar alarm to go off so conveniently? Can you work it out?

Clues: 192/Solution: 258.

THE TRUCK DRIVER

A truck driver was driving along an empty highway when he sensed there was something wrong with his truck. He stopped and got out to look at it. He was then killed. How?

Clues: 211/Solution: 276.

THIRSTY

A man dies of thirst in his own home. How come?

Clues: 209/Solution: 274.

THE CLOTH

A man waved a cloth and another man died. Why?

Clues: 162/Solution: 233.

THE CIRCLE AND THE LINE

They died because the circle crossed the line. Explain.

Clues: 161/Solution: 232.

THE SNIPER

A man is driving in a war zone when he is attacked by a sniper. His car skids and turns over. He manages to crawl out and get behind his car but he is still under fire from the sniper. He has no gun. All he has is a bottle of water, a handkerchief, and a cigarette lighter. How does he escape?

Clues: 203/Solution: 268.

FAIR DEAL

Several truck drivers at a roadside café started to play poker. The pot was large and the game was serious. Suddenly one of the men accused the dealer of cheating. The dealer drew a knife and, in plain view of all the others, stabbed the man and killed him. The police were called and they interviewed everyone who had been present. But no man was arrested or charged with any offense. Why not?

Clues: 169/Solution: 239.

WALLY TEST

Sharpen your pencil and your wits! Here comes a WALLY Test. Write out your answers to these quickfire questions:

1. In Camberley, England, two out of every seven people have telephone numbers that are not listed in the directory. If there are 14,000 names in the Camberley telephone directory, how many of them have numbers that are unlisted?

2. In Iran, a Westerner cannot take a photograph of a man with a turban. Why not?

3. How many successful parachute jumps does a trainee parachutist in the U.S. Army have to make before he graduates from jump school?

4. What is the invention, first discovered in ancient times, that allows people to see through solid walls?

5. A man carefully pointed his car due east and then drove for two miles. He was then two miles west of where he started from. How come?

6. A mail plane was halfway from Dallas to Miami at a height of 2000 feet on a clear, still day. It dropped a 100 kg sack of airmail letters and a 100 kg steel rod at the same time. Which hit the ground first?

7. If two are company and three are a crowd, what are four and five?

8. With which hand does a nun stir her coffee?

9. Why do some people press elevator buttons with their fingers and others with their thumbs?

10. What do you say to a man who claims not to be superstitious?

11. If a grandfather clock strikes thirteen, what time is it?

12. Two sons, two fathers and a grandfather sat together. How many men were there?

13. An archaeologist showed his daughter a coin that he had found on a dig. He told her it was dated 200 B.C. She told him she thought it was a fake. Who was right?

14. For this two-parter, tell us: a) What color is a refrigerator? b) What do cows drink?

See WALLY answers on page 282.

CLUES

The Accident

The driver's car was white. The other car was black.

Acidic Action

He disposed of her clothes and jewelry.

Her body was completely dissolved in acid.

A trace of her was found and identified.

Across the River

They got across without getting wet.

They did not use any additional materials, but crossed the deep, wide river easily.

Adolf Hitler

It was the real Adolf Hitler, the one who led the German Third Reich.

Adolf Hitler was alive at the time, and the war still had much time to run.

The British soldier did not recognize Hitler. But it would have made no difference if he had.

Adrift in the Ocean

They found a source of drinking water.

No rain or ice is involved.

They were in a particular location.

CLUES

∿ After-Shave

He died an accidental death.

He died because his smell was different.

∿ Ageless

They had been involved in an accident. He had aged, but she was perfectly preserved.

∿ Alex Ferguson

Soccer is played in Singapore.

Alex Ferguson's style of coaching would be appropriate.

One of his personal habits would not be acceptable in Singapore.

∿ Alone in a Boat

They were deliberately cast adrift from a famous boat.

The animals can sometimes offend the senses.

∿ Ancient Antics

It has to do with nourishment.

It does not involve a particular strength or physical skill.

It concerns animals.

∿ Angry Response

She was angry because he was late.

They had no particular appointment at eight o'clock.

❧ Another Shooting

The policeman did not shoot the woman deliberately.

The man who was found guilty of the woman's murder had placed her in danger.

The police were trying to save the woman.

❧ Anywhere in the World

The pilot was due to fly from one place to another so that, wherever the passenger wanted to go, it would be on the pilot's route, and dropping the passenger off would hardly make any difference to the pilot's total flight time.

Think of the Earth as a sphere.

❧ The Archaeologist

The item had been removed from the house.

When his wife was away, the archaeologist went for a walk every morning and evening. When she was at home, they took turns going for walks.

❧ The Archduke

He was very vain.

His coat had no buttons or zippers.

❧ Assault and Battery

John is healthy.

The person who hits John does it to help him.

It is a common occurrence.

∾ **The Auction**

He was bidding for a pet.

The creature had a talent.

He thought he was in a competitive auction.

∾ **Axe Attack**

When the woman entered the house she had no idea who the man was and had no intention of doing him any harm.

It was while the woman was in the bathroom that she realized who the man was and decided to kill him.

The woman had seen the axe before.

∾ **The Bad Driver**

Although he always drove badly, he committed no offense in this twenty-year period.

∾ **Bald Facts**

Her hair loss was part of a greater misfortune that befell her.

She did not lose her hair from natural causes.

Her choice of lover was important.

∾ **Bare Bones**

The student was healthy and was not physically abnormal.

She had never had any kind of medical operation.

Every human is born with two femurs.

∿ Barren Patch

The patch of land received the same sunlight and rain as the fertile land around it.

The patch is an irregular shape.

No one had ever gone there, but human action had made the land barren.

∿ Beautiful Girls

He paid in order to get a beautiful girl on each arm.

∿ Below Par

He was not pleased because it was not a good score.

∿ The Big Room

He died because he went back for the brandy.

He drowned.

∿ Biography

His death was accidental.

Had he chosen a different subject for a biography, he would not have died.

The author died a similar death to that suffered by the subject of his biography.

∿ Bombs Away

The bomber was in the air at a height of 20,000 feet and over its target. It was flying right-way-up (unlike a similar, classic puzzle where the pilot could not be having tea). The mechanism was in working order, but the bombs, when released, did not fall from the plane.

The bombs fell.

∿ The Book

He did not buy it for the pictures, illustrations, style, or appearance of the book. Nor did he have any intention of reading it or learning the language it was written in.

He was thrilled to get the book and eager to show it to his friends.

∿ The Bookmark

He has what he considers a better alternative.

∿ The Boss

The boss kept his word, but did not beat the man or back down.

∿ Bostonian

There was nothing strange or unusual about this man.

His friends and neighbors in Boston were also not U.S. citizens.

∾ Bottled Up

The bottles remained unbroken, unchanged, and unused throughout.

They were worthless when empty, but had been expensive when full.

She was status conscious.

∾ Bouncing Baby

The baby was a normal human baby and it fell onto the hard sidewalk, but lived.

∾ The Breeze

He was standing still but moving slowly.

∾ Brunelleschi's Challenge

The table was flat and horizontal. The egg was a regular hen's egg, not cooked or treated in any way. He made the egg stand on the table without any other materials or items.

The other contestants made an assumption about what they were allowed to do. This assumption stopped them from seeing the solution that Brunelleschi used.

∾ Brush-off

Amanda did not invent any excuse or pretense.

She wanted Zoe to think that they had been accidentally interrupted.

CLUES

∾ The Building

He was a thief who had fled.

This took place many years ago.

∾ The Burglary

The neighbor had allowed access in, but had watched every action they made like a hawk.

Something had apparently been delivered in error.

Valuable pictures, which were mounted high on the wall, had not been stolen.

∾ Burnt Wood

The wood has a symbolic value, but is not in itself rare or valuable.

The men involved in this quest all speak English yet come from countries far apart.

They compete over many weeks.

∾ Bus Stop I

The man would have liked to have sat on the chair while he waited for the bus, but he could not.

The man was unhappy, and the chair was the cause of his unhappiness.

When he got on the bus, the man had difficulty paying his fare.

∾ Bus Stop II

The woman does not meet anybody or pass anything of interest or benefit to her by going to the farther bus stop. She does not like exercise.

When the woman comes home, she walks to the nearer bus stop in order to catch the bus.

The woman finds it easier to walk two hundred yards from the far bus stop, rather than one hundred yards from the near bus stop.

∾ Business Rivalry

Cain uses Abel's lower prices to his own personal advantage.

Cain changes his profession.

They were competitors in the early days of the railroad business.

∾ By the River

The man had intended to fire the gun.

No one was in danger.

He would not have used the gun if he had not been near the river.

∾ Bypass

In this true incident, trucks continued to pour through the town, although cars used the new road.

∾ Call Box

She gave the telephone company a strong incentive to fix
the call box.

She told the telephone company that some people were very
pleased that the telephone did not work properly.

∾ Capsize

It overbalanced when the weight distribution on the boat
suddenly changed.

Something quite light dropped onto one side of the boat.

∾ Car in the River

He did not have any special equipment or powers.

He breathed normally throughout the whole incident.

∾ The Carpet Seller

The solution can be accomplished in a single cut, but it is
not a straight cut.

The two pieces can fit together perfectly to make either a
nine by sixteen rectangle or a twelve by twelve square.

The carpet is not used on the stairs, but it may be helpful to
think in terms of steps!

Cartoon Character

The scientific journal misstated and exaggerated the properties of something.

The cartoon character was designed to be a sort of role model for children, and to influence their habits.

The cartoon character was intended to make an unpopular but healthy item popular.

The Cartoonist

The cartoonist is employed to draw cartoons, but not for entertainment or amusement.

The cartoons are used in pilot training.

Cash in Hand

Smith offered to pay Jones the thousand dollars at a time when it would have been disadvantageous for Jones to accept it.

Whichever of them had the money would lose it shortly.

Catching a Bullet

The second man had no special powers or protection. However, in each solution he would need very precise positioning.

The bullet is a normal bullet fired from a normal gun and is normally deadly.

When the man catches the bullet, it is travelling slowly.

∿ **Chimney Problem**

He came down very slowly.

The chimney was not the same after he finished his descent.

∿ **The Cicada**

It is thought that the 17-year life cycle of the cicada gives it additional protection against predators. But it is not safer underground than any other such grub, nor safer as an insect than any other cicada.

∿ **The Circle and the Line**

They died an accidental death in the course of a journey.

They could see the line drawing nearer. However, the line never moved.

∿ **The Circular Table**

She solved the problem easily and without special equipment.

She used a piece of paper.

∿ **Circular Tour**

What we think of as equal are often not equal.

∿ **Clean Shaven**

Alexander the Great was interested in military conquest.

He believed that clean-shaven soldiers had an advantage.

∾ The Climber

He hid the boots, but in a way that, even if they were found, it was unlikely they would be taken.

They were a fine pair of climbing boots.

∾ The Clinch

Something caused them to be locked together even though they wanted to part.

∾ The Cloth

The man who waved the cloth knew that his action would probably cause a man to die.

He did not know which man would die.

The man died of a gunshot.

∾ The Code

The members and the doorman were consistent and logical in what they said and did. There was a code based solely on the numbers, which they followed.

The code would work in other languages but probably with different combinations of numbers. (For example, in Italian the doorman might say "Otto" and the member reply, "Quattro.")

∾ Complete Garbage

If the garbage had not been emptied, he would have lived.

He was poor and tired.

He died a violent death.

∿ Confectionery Manufacturer

The confectionery is a popular and healthy food.

The workers are always very busy.

∿ The Container

It was a common article then and now.

∿ The Courtier

The courtier did not have any particular musical skill, but he had a good memory.

The king had a particular affliction.

The courtier was called into use on certain state occasions.

∿ Cowardly Act

He risked pain and physical injury because he thought that he might thereby avoid a greater risk.

He hoped to get shot.

∿ The Crash

The police were not surprised that they could not find any drivers for the cars.

No one had left the scene of the accident.

∿ Creepy Crawlies

He poisoned the bugs.

The places he went gave him what was worthless to them but useful to him.

∿ Cross the Gorge

This happened over a hundred years ago, before planes or rockets could be used. The engineers could cross the gorge only by travelling miles downstream.

Just as the world's entire population is descended from Adam and Eve, so a small beginning can lead to a great outcome.

∿ The Cruel King

The king did not punish the men for any wrongdoing on their part, but rather for his own selfish reasons.

Their punishment was execution. It meant that they could never present a threat to the king.

The king was miserly, selfish, cruel, and very rich.

∿ Dali's Brother

Salvador Dali is recognized as a brilliant surrealist painter.

Salvador Dali's younger brother was actually a brilliant surrealist painter but his older brother never knew this.

The two brothers had something important and unusual in common.

∿ Dance Ban

The other contestants thought he used a low trick, but it was really just a natural advantage in this kind of dance.

∿ A Day at the Races

The man deserved to be punished.

He had no special influence with the police, and they fully intended to prosecute him.

He had a special skill that he often used to his advantage.

∿ Dead Drunk

He died an accidental death as a result of his actions and where he was.

He was alone at a subway station.

∿ Dead Man, Dead Dog

The man had been fishing illegally in a lake.

In desperation the man had run away from the lake, but to no avail.

The dog was a retriever.

∿ The Deadly Climb

Climbing conditions were perfect as the men all walked up the high mountain. The dead man's companions were unharmed, but he died a painful death.

The man was an enthusiastic, all-round sportsman. He climbed the mountain in the afternoon.

It was what the man did in the morning which led to his death on the mountain.

∿ The Deadly Diamonds

The thief did not use any special powers or materials to subdue or control the snakes.

The thief opened the box in a way which allowed him to safely extract the diamonds.

∿ The Deadly Melody

She was in her home when this happened.

She had heard the tune many times before. Normally she was happy when she heard this tune.

The stranger was trying to rob her.

∿ Debugging

Ants were used in the diagnosis of diabetes.

The ants' actions could indicate that a person had diabetes.

∿ Depressurization

He did this for his own safety.

The rattle alerted him to a problem which might become dangerous.

∿ Desert

People need to have water in their bodies in order to survive. How did the man get it?

No other person or creature is involved.

He did not find liquids of any kind in the desert.

∽ Doctor's Appointment

> The doctor and the woman had never met and there was no prior connection between them.
>
> The doctor was embarrassed when he found out why the woman was there.
>
> The doctor was trying to create a good impression on his first day.

∽ Dogs Home

> The truck had two doors at the back.
>
> One door was open and one was closed.

∽ Don't Get Up

> No one else is in the apartment and she knows that no one else will answer the phone.
>
> She does not know the caller, but she knows that the call is probably important.
>
> She knows the call is not for her.
>
> She has no malicious motives.

∽ A Door Too Large

> He had to take two cuts from the door to make it fit. Both cuts were from the length of the door. The width and thickness remained the same.

∾ The Drive

They had never done this before, but once they started they followed this same procedure for several weeks: swapping places where the drive met the road. Then they never did it again.

∾ Dud Car

The Nova had a poor image, even though it was a good automobile.

People laughed when they heard of it.

∾ 88 Too Big

It was a number he chose to use.

He was not at home.

He did not know the right number.

∾ Elevator

She was not alone in the elevator.

There was a misunderstanding.

∾ The End of the War

An unusual event marked the end of the war. It is an event that nowadays we can date with great precision.

∿ The Engineer

He stood on the river bank watching the dam, which was in excellent condition.

He was killed accidentally by one of the dam's constructors.

Although he had heard about this kind of dam before, he had never seen one and he marvelled at its construction. No mechanical aids or formal training had been used.

∿ Exceptional Gratitude

Bill thanked Ted for eggs he had never received in order to influence Ted's actions.

They were neighbors.

Ted was lazy and mean.

∿ Export Drive

They relocated their premises within Japan.

They made a true but misleading statement on their goods.

∿ Fair Deal

There was nothing faked or pretended about this incident. The dealer had murdered the man who was stabbed.

The dealer was punished for the crime.

∿ Fair Fight

The boxer did not expect to collect any money.

The trainer collected a worthwhile sum for his efforts.

The boxer won fairly, but without throwing a punch.

∾ The Fall

The man had no special skills or training. Many other people can do this.

Some people find this kind of fall enjoyable. Others are terrified.

∾ Fall of the Hall

No animal activity or change in the state of the building components or structure is involved.

It had been used for a different purpose than that for which it was designed.

∾ Fall of the Wall

The construction of the wall was sound. It did not have any structural or mechanical weaknesses.

The wall was breached through subtlety rather than through force.

∾ The Farmer

He had had no intention of ploughing up the field until he had awoken that morning.

He ruined the crops in the forlorn hope of a much larger harvest.

He was superstitious.

∾ Fill Her Up!

He deliberately ruined the car, but later he deeply regretted his action.

He was a jealous cement truck driver.

∾ Fingerprint Evidence

It was not Bundy's fingerprints or any of his victim's fingerprints that incriminated him, but it was fingerprint evidence.

The police found something unusual when they searched Bundy's apartment.

∾ Fired for Joining Mensa

Anne's employers would not have objected to her joining any other organization.

She was employed in an administrative position, she did her job well, and her employers were pleased with her.

If she had joined Mensa, there may have been a conflict of interest.

∾ 500 Times

This is a physical difference and, for the purposes of the puzzle, it may be assumed that Florence and Washington are about the same size and age.

CLUES

∾ Flipping Pages

I did this deliberately in order to produce a specific result.

I could do this only in certain places.

I should have gotten permission from the publisher first.

∾ The Forger

He was nearly arrested for a driving offense that very
morning.

∾ The Forgery

There was nothing wrong with the general appearance of
the document, the paper it was on, or the signature of the
king.

The date on the document indicated to the expert that it
was a forgery.

The date was a day in 1752, which would appear normal to
many people. The expert knew that the document could
not have been printed or signed on that particular date.

∾ 40 Feet Ahead

He was a normal man who walked in a normal fashion.

It was a long walk.

CLUES

∾ Free Lunch

The man ate his lunch with one knife and one fork.

He provided a service.

The restaurant provided an intimate atmosphere in the evenings.

∾ Full Refund

It was highly unusual for the theater to give a refund.

The theater manager was glad that they left.

They had acted cruelly.

∾ Garbage Nosiness

I was annoyed with myself, not with my neighbors.

I looked in the cans on the same morning each week.

When I looked in the cans, I saw that they had something in common, which mine did not.

∾ Gas Attack

He did not use the mask to disguise himself or anyone else.

The gas mask was standard issue.

His actions could have saved the lives of many people.

∾ Gaze Away

The man was physically normal, yet he was different from all the other people.

Everyone treated him with great respect.

CLUES

∿ Getting Away with Murder

The man had a long-standing motive to kill her.

He was clearly guilty, but had to be released under the law.

He was punished for this crime.

∿ The Golden Vase

He hid in a small broom closet near the vase.

He came from Australia.

He convinced the guards that the alarm was faulty.

∿ Golf Bag

Paul removed the bag without touching it.

He did not deliberately set fire to the bag since that would have incurred a penalty.

He indulged in a bad habit.

∿ The Golfer

He was playing regular golf in which one plays from tee to green and tries to do so in the fewest strokes.

His previous shot had been a very poor one.

∿ Good-bye, Mother

The old lady had a mean purpose in mind when she asked the young woman the favor.

∾ Grease

The man had a benevolent purpose in mind and the stranger was pleased to have the grease rubbed all over his head.

The man was in uniform, the stranger was not.

∾ Great Detection

The police examined all clues left at the scene of the crime and quickly knew where they could find the robber.

∾ The Great Wall

He had travelled a long way to see a sight that very few people have seen.

∾ A Hairy Story

No wigs, potions, or transplants were involved.

After her actions, his hair looked exactly like hers.

∾ Happy Birthday

There was nothing about his appearance that indicated it was his birthday.

He was not well known.

She worked in a shop but was not a shop assistant.

She had access to information.

The Hasty Packer

She packed one essential item for a particular kind of journey.

She packed material and string.

The Hasty Robber

The other gun was not in the bank.

He was apprehended by the police. But not for robbery.

Headline News

The editor of the newspaper had not known what the jury's verdict would be, but he ensured that his newspaper was available, with the correct headline and story, as soon as the trial finished.

Heartless

The man's profession is important.

The Helicopter

It was a real helicopter hovering over a real sea. The helicopter stopped flying and stopped hovering, but it did not hit the sea.

The helicopter was owned by an oil company.

Hide-and-Seek

Jackie's condition had changed such that she was now much easier to find. John had a disability which gave him no advantage in finding Jackie.

CLUES

∾ **High Blood Pressure**

Gerald's blood pressure is normal for Gerald.

∾ **Hole in One**

She hit one shot and her ball finished in the hole, but this did not count as a hole in one.

∾ **Holy Orders**

The priest was a real priest carrying a real gun. He was not a criminal and no crime was involved.

He wanted to shoot something.

The gun was used to solve an unsightly problem.

∾ **Homecoming**

The cost of transporting the goods home was very high. The company claimed that the executive had misled them over what he wanted to bring back, but he showed the court that he had been accurate in his description.

∾ **Homing Spaniards**

They did not mark the path in any particular way, nor did they memorize the route.

They rode out and rode back. No other people, birds, or animals served as guides.

Some of them rode stallions, but certainly not all of them did.

CLUES

∾ Hosing Down

They used regular water. The road was not contaminated in any way.

It was for a special event.

They did not hose the entire road.

∾ Houdini's Challenge

He did not use any special equipment or explosive. He knew that he could not unlock the safe using a conventional approach, so he used a lateral approach.

Although the safe manufacturer and onlookers witnessed the feat, they could not see how Houdini managed to unlock the safe door.

∾ How to Choose a Builder

He had no knowledge of building or of the builders' experience.

He did not decide on price. He wanted a reliable builder of good reputation and quality.

He enlisted the help of the builders in selecting one who met his requirements.

∾ The Impostor

The woman answered all their questions faultlessly and
agreed to undergo any tests they requested.

The real Anastasia had a medical condition that would not
have been immediately apparent even to a doctor. The
woman underwent no medical tests.

Her agreement to take a test was seen as evidence that she
was an impostor.

∾ Invaluable

The man was a criminal.

He was both lucky and unlucky.

∾ The Investigator

The private investigator had a camera.

The man was under investigation for fraud.

The investigator was gathering evidence for an insurance
company.

∾ Invisible

It can be made of metal or wood.

It is powerful.

You can see it under some circumstances, but not others,
even when it is directly in front of you.

CLUES

◇ Jam Doughnut

He was in a foreign city.

◇ Job Description

She acted on impulse, but she chose them for a specific reason.

The woman was angry because of the men's actions.

She knew they had been talking about her.

◇ Job Lot

They had been designed for a specific purpose.

They would be very useful for one type of building.

◇ Keys in the Car

The man did not mean to lock his keys in the car. He had no criminal or ulterior motive. It was an accident.

When he had been unable to retrieve his keys, the man had initiated another course of action in order to get them.

◇ Kid Stuff

The expert's theory has nothing to do with the behavior of children.

It has to do with the appearance of children to the motorist.

∾ Large and Small

All the groups of people were engaged in the same activity.

The large, fit people were chosen for their strength. The small people were chosen for their light weight and their judgment.

∾ Leadfoot and Gumshoe

She and the police officer were strangers and she was not trying to help or impress him.

She was acting from high moral principles, and was also protecting someone's reputation.

∾ The Less-Costly Capital

The city spends less in this service area than other cities because it has less need to spend.

The service on which this capital city spends less is firefighting.

The city is not particularly cold or damp, yet its geography makes fires less likely.

∾ Library Lunacy

The library benefited from this temporary change in the rules.

This relaxation of the normal rules of borrowing was a one-time event caused by something else which was happening at the library.

∾ The Lifeboat

He was not rescued during the two days, nor did he see land or any other refuge.

The lifeboat was old-fashioned in design and construction.

∾ Light Saving

The only thing that was changed was the design of the lightbulb and its socket.

The bulbs could still be removed by hand by the city engineers and maintenance staff.

The bulbs could be reached by hand by anyone, but the vandals found that, try as they might to unscrew the bulbs, they could not remove them.

∾ The Lumberjacks

During his breaks, Joe does something which helps him to cut more trees.

∾ Machine Forge

The man sells the machine to a crook.

Although the machine produces perfect $100 bills, it cannot be used to make the crook rich.

∾ Man in Tights

He was knocked out by the rock, but it did not touch him.

He was involved in many dangerous adventures.

He was a well-known sight in his tights.

∿ Man Overboard

The previous day he had bought some beautiful postcards of Jerusalem.

∿ The Man Who Got Water

He had intended to use the water in connection with his car, but something happened to make him change his mind.

He was very angry.

∿ The Man Who Returned Too Soon

He died an accidental death. No other person or creature was involved.

The danger was not in his home. What killed him was the fact that he returned too quickly.

∿ The Man Who Shot Himself

The man shot himself with his own gun and with the immediate intention of killing himself. He had no history of suicidal tendencies, insanity, phobias, or psychological disorders.

The two men met shortly before the man shot himself. No words were spoken when they met, but because of the murderer's actions the man shot himself.

Both men were gangsters.

∾ Matchless

The individual was the first person ever to have been born under certain circumstances.

From a medical or biological point of view, there was nothing unusual about the person's birth.

The location of the person's birth was singular.

∾ Mickey Mouse's Girlfriend

It was a deadly serious exercise.

It was a test.

∾ The Millionaire

The man is very famous.

The sandwiches that were left out were eaten by a visitor whose actions inspired the man.

He could draw very well.

∾ The Missing Diamond

An enterprising thief had worked out a way of figuring out the combination.

The thief had left something in the room.

∾ Missing Items

He grows them.

Everyone has them—men and women.

They are in the lower part of the body.

∾ The Missing Money

Nobody else was involved. At the end of the first day there was $170 in his trouser pocket. The next day he had $5 in his trouser pocket.

∾ Misunderstood

Very few, if any, criminals speak this language.

It is chosen for its rarity.

A handful of words are used—but they are important.

∾ Motion Not Passed

Many people voted for the motion, and the poll was performed correctly according to the rules.

If a few more people had voted against the motion, it would have been passed. If many more people had voted against it, then it would have been rejected.

∾ Motionless

He was a perfectly healthy person and free to move, but he sat still voluntarily.

There was another person in the room. He was performing a service for the first man, but they never touched.

This took place during the nineteenth century.

∾ Murder

The police discovered that she had been poisoned. They checked all the food and drink in the house and could find no trace of poison.

She had bought many fine plates, but rarely went to shops or markets.

The day before her death she had been to the grocery store and the post office.

∾ Murder in the Newspaper

His profession is important.

He had met the murderer.

∾ Mutilation

The man was a criminal.

He hoped to escape detection.

∾ A Mysterious Death

The man died an accidental but highly unusual death.

There was a tiny hole in his head.

Thousands fly through the air, but very few reach the ground.

∾ New Shoes

She died because she wore the new shoes.

She was involved in entertainment.

∾ No More Bore

Churchill gave the butler something.

The butler gave the impression that he was misbehaving.

∾ No Response

The question was one that he often answered, and if anyone else had asked it he would have answered.

The content of the question does not matter. It was the way it was asked that matters.

The stranger had a difficulty.

∾ The Nonchalant Police Officer

He was not cowardly or neglecting his duty.

No one else in the street took any notice of the robbers, even though they were seen by several passers-by.

∾ The Nonchalant Wife

Even though she found her husband's remains on the floor, the woman had no reason to call any authorities.

The woman was horrified to see her husband's remains on the floor, but not at all surprised that he was dead.

∾ Nonconventional

They are not prohibited from speaking altogether.

The do not use signs, gestures, or codes.

They are extremely courteous and concerned for the well-being of their companions.

Nonexistent Actors

The nonexistent actors had never existed and took no part whatsoever in the movie, but their names were put deliberately into the credits.

It was a murder-mystery movie.

The Nosy Student

Judy hid her letters in the shared room, but in a rather good hiding place.

The roommate was a very poor student.

Noteworthy

The criminal had committed a crime in the woman's house.

The criminal had visited the bank.

The picture of the president is well known.

November 11

Although it appeared as though many customers had been born on November 11, the real distribution of births of the company's customers was not unusual.

All the data had been entered on a computer database.

The customers appeared to have birthdays on November 11, 1911.

Nun-plussed

The doctor smiled and explained that he had cured the nun's complaint.

∾ An Odd Number

You need no mathematical skills to solve this problem.

Note that each digit is used once.

The sequence of the digits is significant.

∾ Once Too Often

You can do this many times in your life.

You do it on a specific day that is not of your choosing.

It is variously considered a right, a privilege, and a duty.

∾ One Inch Shorter

The man was fit and healthy, as was necessary for his
    physically demanding job.

Nothing was cut off the man—he became an inch shorter as
    a result of an incident at work.

He was subjected to enormous forces.

∾ One Mile

The one-mile kink is not associated with any physical or
    geographical feature of the landscape. The land there is
    the same as elsewhere along the border.

There was no mistake in the original map and none in the
    current map.

Actions were taken to speed up the survey of the border.

CLUES

∽ Orange Trick

The second orange goes under the first orange but the first orange remains on the table.

∽ Paddle Your Own Canoe

The man and the canoe were normal, but the river was unusual.

He could do this only at a certain time of year.

∽ Page 78

She was not looking for a particular book, but for books in general that were interesting and new.

Her husband read the books.

∽ The Painter

He was a very good painter whose work could be seen at art galleries and private houses.

He was not shy of publicity and he used his own name.

He did not paint on canvas.

∽ The Painting

She tried not to hurt his feelings.

She claimed to like and understand the painting.

∽ The Parcel

It was something that she made for someone else.

She knew it would probably be found and handed in.

∾ Pass Protection

Other people could pass through in the same fashion that I did.

As I looked at the people in line, I could see the frustration in their faces.

I always buy a token for every journey.

∾ Pentagon Panic

This has nothing to do with technology, rocket design, wind, or weather.

The same missile would get from Moscow to New York faster than it would get from New York to Moscow. If missiles were launched by both countries at the same time, the Russian missile would strike first. The reverse would be true for the same missiles going from Alaska to Vladivostock in eastern Russia. Then, the American missile would strike first.

∾ Pentagon Puzzle

The number of people working there is not relevant.

The reason dates back to when the Pentagon was built.

When it was built, the extra bathrooms were necessary.

∾ The Perfect Murder

He had caused something to fall so that its motion would be detected by the burglar alarm sensors.

No electrical, telephone, or radio devices were used. He did not use any spring or complex mechanical device. He used something much simpler.

∾ Picture Purchase

He was honest and there were no crooked motives involved.

He did not intend to take any action to make the picture more valuable.

He would not have bought the picture if it had been rolled up.

∾ The Pilot's Son

No stepfathers, grandparents, or in-law relationships are involved. The passenger was the father of the pilot's son.

∾ Point-Blank Shot

The gun was a real handgun in full working order, firing real bullets that would normally kill someone.

She was the kind of person who would make every effort to improve her career.

∾ Poisoned

He had followed his normal daily routine unaware that someone had planned to poison him. He had met no one else on the day of his murder.

He had inadvertently put the poison into his mouth.

∾ Police Visit

The purpose of the police visit has nothing to do with your driving skill or the condition of the car.

The population of Tokyo is over sixteen million people.

∾ Poor Delivery

The misunderstanding was based on a problem with written communication. Each company followed exactly the same written instructions but interpreted them differently.

∾ Poor Dogs

They had trained the dogs with the intention of inflicting harm on enemies.

The dogs did exactly what they had been trained to do.

∾ Poor Equipment

The piece of equipment was a watch.

The man took it somewhere on Earth where there is no official time.

∾ Poor Impersonation

The actress was found out because she had used a mirror to rehearse.

Her voice was faultless. She looked exactly like the heiress in all regards except one.

∾ Poor Investment

They could easily buy another of these items; in fact, they had several spare ones.

If it was lost, then it had to be found.

They were looking for information.

∾ The Postman

He did not use anything to distract the dog except himself.

∾ The Power of Tourism

The tourists do not consume large amounts of electricity.

The place does not have costly lights or unusual electrical entertainment or appliances.

The place is a famous natural tourist attraction.

∾ Precognition

The profession of the lady who knocked at the door is important.

∿ The Professors

The two professors each saw a simple written equation. But, for a very basic reason, they saw it differently. This made it right for one, but wrong for the other.

As they argued about this they looked straight at each other.

∿ Promotion

The company knows exactly what John is like.

Promoting John is part of a clever plan.

They promote him very publicly.

∿ The Quatorzième

His work consists of eating a meal in a restaurant.

He always eats in a large group, but generally with people he has never met before and has nothing particularly in common with.

∿ Radio Broadcast

The high-pitched noise achieved its intended purpose of driving off mosquitoes while being inaudible to humans.

∿ Radio Death

He had been expecting to hear the piece of music that he heard, but had not planned to commit suicide.

There was something about the way the music was playing which meant that he was in very serious trouble.

∾ The Ransom Note

The police could glean no clues from the content, paper, or style of the ransom note.

The ransom note was mailed, but the postmark gave no clues.

There were no fingerprints, but the police were able to establish a unique match with the criminal.

∾ Rare Event

This is not an astronomical, geological or physical event.

The answer relates to the date. It last happened in the days of the Beatles and John F. Kennedy.

∾ Recovery

There was nothing wrong with the tow truck. The truck that had broken down had a serious fault which was remedied by the way they drove back.

∾ Red Light

The police officer was perfectly capable of chasing the teenagers and he was not engaged in any other task at the time.

The officer was conscientious and always chased and apprehended those he saw breaking the law.

∾ Reentry

It is popular.

It is a collection.

∾ Regular Arguments

It was the same topic and conversation which led them to
quarrel every night.

On Saturdays they argued in the afternoon as well.

∾ Rejected Shoes

The shoes fit him comfortably, but there was something
uncomfortable about them.

They were made of different material from his other shoes.

They were fine when worn outside, but not when worn
inside.

∾ Replacing the Leaves

The girl is very sad.

She is trying to prevent something from happening.

She is acting on something she heard.

∾ A Riddle

He had sight and he took fruit.

∾ Riddle of the Sphinx

The Sphinx had poetic license. Morning, afternoon, and
evening are metaphorical rather than literal times.

Not all the legs are limbs, but they all support the body.

∾ **Right Off**

He is upset that his new car is ruined, but pleased at
    something else.

No other vehicle is involved.

He acquires something rare.

∾ **Robbery**

The gang did not attempt to flee. They thought laterally.
    The police did not.

∾ **The Rock**

He was uninjured, but the rock damaged his suit.

∾ **The Runner**

He knew that he had reached the end of the race, but he
    kept on running because he had a good reason to run.

∾ **Russian Racer**

The papers reported accurately, but put the most positive
    light on the Russian car's performance and the most
    negative on the American car's.

The papers did not report how many cars raced.

∾ **Sacrifice**

They did not choose by chance but agreed between them
    based on a good reason, which even the one chosen had
    to admit was sound.

They had different beliefs and philosophies.

∿ The Salesman

There was nothing wrong with the vacuum cleaner. It was in perfect working order.

He had had a long drive to reach the house.

∿ School Friend

Joe did not know who had married his friend. He had no other source of information than this conversation.

He knew that the girl's mother was called Louise.

∿ Scuba Do

He had not been diving and had no immediate intention of going diving.

He was an avid diver.

The reason had to do with safety.

∿ Secret Assignment

Knowing the students' habits, he did some clever detective work.

He knew they were serious, studious, and always prepared themselves for assignments.

He checked something in a particular place at the university.

∿ The Secretary

She had taken a key. She posted it back immediately.

She was dismissed because she posted it back.

∿ Sell More Beer

The consultant gave the bar owner a piece of advice that many of the bar's customers would have been glad to hear.

Implementing the advice would benefit the customers more than the bar owner.

∿ The Service

The man paid more than others for the same service in the expectation of future gain.

The man was a collector.

∿ Seven Bells

The shopkeeper could easily change the sign, but chooses not to do so.

No superstition about numbers is involved.

Many people notice the discrepancy.

∿ Shaking a Fist

The man was not a criminal. He had been driving erratically.

There was something unusual about the man.

The policeman quickly knew that the man was in danger.

∿ A Shooting

Rob was not a police officer, nor was he acting in self-defense. Bill was not a criminal. His murder was in no way justified.

Rob had had no intention of killing Bill. The police were satisfied that someone other than Rob was the murderer.

Their professions are important.

∿ Shooting a Dead Man

The policeman knew that the man was already dead.

He wanted someone else to see what he was doing.

He was not tampering with evidence. He was trying to get information.

∿ The Shoplifter

She does not stop, because she is in danger of being caught.

She steals under a certain guise that enables her to gradually steal larger items.

She is recognized on her regular circuit, but is not known to be a shoplifter.

∿ The Sign

The sign was inside the car and the car was stationary.

He shot her because he learned she had been having an affair.

The Signal

John did not have any special extrasensory or psychic powers.

James received the signal, but not by sight or touch or feel.

John often went out with James for a walk together.

Six-Foot Drop

The tomato fell six feet.

It was a regular tomato.

The man was fast.

Slow Drive

There is nothing wrong with the man, the car, the road, or the driving conditions.

This happened under very particular circumstances. At other times he drives at normal speeds.

If he went faster, he would lose something he values.

The Slow-Car Race

The desert and the full fuel tanks are not important here. What is important is that the last car back wins the race for its owner. The driver raced back in order to win the race.

Small Furniture

They make the furniture for a special kind of house.

The furniture is seen by many but used by very few.

∿ Smart Appearance

Professional help had been involved in making Victor look particularly smart.

Everyone noticed how smart he looked but no one spoke to him.

∿ The Sniper

The sniper is determined to shoot him and will come to the car to do so if he takes cover.

Attack is the best form of defense.

∿ A Solution of Paint

The problem concerned transportation. The use of the paint stopped the problem of overloading.

∿ Space Shuttle

This has nothing to do with the materials that the space shuttle is made of, nor with the radio communications.

The direction of the shuttle's flight and the nature of its exhaust are relevant.

∾ Speeding

The police officers would have liked to book the man, but they could not. Both officers had given out several other speeding tickets that day, and they were eager to do it again.

The man was not a doctor or a diplomat. He had no good excuse or exemption.

The answer relates to jurisdiction. Although the man had clearly committed an offense, and although a police officer with jurisdiction was present to give out speeding tickets, the man could not be given a ticket.

∾ Speeding Ticket

It was not a one-way street and there was nothing wrong or unusual about the car.

He was breaking the general speed limit.

∾ Spraying the Grass

He wanted the grass to look perfect.

Something was different about the spraying this time.

If he had done this regularly, it would eventually have harmed the grass.

∾ Stand at the Back

There was an emergency and passengers were in danger.

It had nothing to do with how the plane was flying or with weight distribution.

∿ **The Statue**

No ramps, slides, or levers were used. The statue was not tilted or dropped.

The statue was lowered using ropes. The ropes were removed. The statue then settled very slowly onto the base.

∿ **Statue of an Insect**

The insect had caused a big problem.

The town's prosperity depends on agriculture.

The insect's actions caused a change.

∿ **Steer Clear of the Banks**

Roller-blading, cycling and running were all forbidden on the road.

∿ **The Stiff Gate**

The host was a famous inventor and engineer.

The guests, in pushing open the gate, were performing a useful job for the host.

∿ **The Stockbroker**

He sent out many predictions, but he was not a good predictor.

∿ **Stolen Finger**

He wanted to send it to someone.

He wanted someone to think it was his finger.

∽ Stop/Go

The individuals are not color-blind or disabled in any way.

Their purpose and approach is serious and includes the use of a stopwatch, pencil, and paper.

From time to time the people change one aspect of the vehicle they are driving.

∽ Straight Ahead

It was not done for economic reasons.

The straight miles make no difference to traffic conditions.

The straight miles were designed for use in extreme circumstances.

∽ Strange Reactions

Joan was pleased at the news of her promotion. John was disappointed to learn that he was losing his job.

The nature of their work is important.

∽ Strangulation

She was strangled to death with a scarf.

No dancing was involved.

She should not have been in such a hurry.

∽ Striking the Elephant

The man is very skillful in his use of the stick.

The man strikes something made of ivory.

∿ Stringing Along

He used the string in a competition.

He gained an unfair advantage over his rivals.

∿ The Suitcase and the Box

He had gained his freedom but lost something dear to him.

The suitcase and the box had contained the personal belongings he had had for several years.

The smaller building was a bar into which he had gone to celebrate and to show off the contents of the box.

∿ Suspense

This was a regular occurrence on this particular railway. It allows an essential change to take place.

Although the rail car being lifted so high in the air does shock new passengers, the reason for this action is not difficult for them to gauge.

∿ Sweet in Pocket

The man noticed that the sweet in his pocket was affected by something with which he was experimenting.

The invention is used in cooking.

∿ Sweet Wheat

His primary concern is to ensure that his wheat will be of the finest quality.

He is quite happy for his neighbors to grow his strain of wheat and thereby produce better wheat. He gains by this.

∿ The Swimmer

There was nothing amiss with the pool, the water, or the ambient conditions. The problem of recognizing the time concerned Sylvia Ester.

She was a well-known swimmer who had won many other events in recognized times. But there was something different about her swim this day.

∿ T-Shirts

The T-shirts were designed to circumvent the law.

The law was a traffic regulation.

The black band was a diagonal stripe.

∿ Talking to Herself

The man was recording something for his archives.

She held a unique distinction.

∿ **Teenage Party**

> The boy and the house gave no clue to the fact that the boy had been drinking.
>
> The place where the gin was kept is relevant.
>
> The father did not like a lot of ice in his gin and tonic.

∿ **The Test**

> Each boy deserved the grade he was given.
>
> There was something unusual about the test.
>
> Jerry was not as diligent as he should have been.

∿ **Third Place**

> It was an acting contest.
>
> The man was a famous actor and movie star.
>
> The contest was for fun.

∿ **Thirsty**

> The man was fit and not hampered in his movements.
>
> There was plenty of water in and near his home.

∿ **Three Notes**

> She had never met any of the three people and had no intention of meeting them, but her note was a serious communication.
>
> The bank robber was part of a gang and had a specific role in the planned robbery.
>
> The Bolivian was a tourist.

∾ Three Spirals

It appeared as though she was receiving something for pleasure, but for her it was deadly serious.

She was involved in dangerous and illegal activities.

The spirals contained information.

∾ Time of Arrival

The mother deduced correctly from what she saw that he must have gotten home very late.

When he came in, the boy did not make a sound. He removed his boots and then crept up to bed.

∾ Title Role

She had been given the role of a beautiful and successful woman.

The book is by Daphne du Maurier. It concerns a woman who dies under mysterious circumstances.

∾ Too Polite

The polite man did not say anything. He simply made a very polite action at an unfortunate time.

He was in a large office, going from one department to another.

∾ The Tower

There were no safety nets, ladders, or scaffolding. If he had jumped from the other side of the building, he would have been killed.

CLUES

∿ The Tree and the Axe

She used the axe to destroy the tree that she had recently bought.

She did not buy the tree in order to put it into the garden.

∿ The Trial

The prosecutor had arranged for the announcement of the missing man's "return," knowing full well that it would not happen.

The accused man knew that the missing man could not return.

∿ The Truck Driver

He was killed accidentally. No other person or creature was involved.

He had sensed that something was wrong with his truck. He was right. His death and the problem with the truck were linked.

∿ The Twelve

The twelve people who have achieved this feat were all men. They were not especially rich or influential or exceptionally talented, but they were intensively trained.

The twelve people who have done this all did it within a ten-year period in the 1960s and 1970s.

∿ Twin Trouble

They were normal natural twins.

Bob was born first. The birth certificate correctly showed Sam's time of birth as before Bob's.

∿ Two Clocks

They were fully functional clocks that were used to measure time.

The clocks were used only occasionally and never when the man was on his own.

The man had a particular hobby.

∿ The Two Drivers

Although the two drivers had driven in identical fashion, one had committed an offense and the other had not. The police officer acted properly.

It happened in a hot country.

∿ Two Jugs

There was no divider in the vat; it was one large container.

After the pourings, the vat contained all the lemonade and all the milk—yet they were separate.

If you could have heard the operation, you would know the answer.

∿ Two Men

The death of one man resulted in a benefit to the other.

The man who was happy was not responsible for the other man's death, but he knew exactly when it would happen.

∿ Two Suitcases

He does not intend to carry the suitcase far.

He is trying to save money.

∿ The Typist

She was chosen on merit.

She was a good typist.

∿ The Unbroken Arm

She was not seeking sympathy or help. Nothing was concealed in the cast.

She was about to do something important.

She knew that the plaster cast would be noticed immediately.

∿ Unclimbed

It is not underwater—it is clearly visible aboveground.

It would be very difficult to climb.

～ The Unhappy Patient

The doctor took an X-ray.

The patient was warned that "anything found may be used in evidence against you."

～ Unknown Recognition

The man was physically normal and there was nothing abnormal about his appearance.

I am not related to him, but a relationship is involved.

～ The Unlucky Bed

All the patients who died were seriously ill, but they were not expected to die.

There is nothing wrong or dangerous about the bed or its location.

No doctors or nurses are involved in the cause of the deaths.

Patients receiving particular treatment are put in this bed.

～ The Unlucky Gambler

He had drawn a ticket from the hat but it did not bear the number 77. The only things that his friends had put in the hat were tickets with the number 77.

～ The Unsuccessful Robbery

Their timing was very poor.

The bank had had plenty of money at the start of the day.

∾ Untying the Ropes

Ropes were not involved in the way the man died, nor was he tied up in the ropes.

Untying the ropes was a form of signal.

∾ Up in the Air

It is small.

It does not fly.

Check your assumptions on every word of the puzzle!

∾ Vanishing Point

The place the man wanted to go to is well known, but very few people go there.

The man was taken to the famous place and saw what he expected. He later discovered that it had not really been the famous place, but no one had deceived him.

The place is marked, but it is not on land.

∾ The Ventriloquist

The ventriloquist could do much better tricks with one dummy than with his other dummies.

Walking Backward

There was no one else in the house.

The man was not afraid of any danger to himself.

He did not know who had rung the bell.

He ran out the back in order to run around to the front of the house.

Waterless Rivers

This is not a physical place.

It has mountains, but you could walk over them easily.

The cities, forests, mountains, and rivers are real places on planet Earth.

Weak Case

He paid his bail fully and promptly, but paying it incriminated him.

He paid in cash, but it was untraceable.

Well Dressed

She was not cold and did not need to wear her hat and coat.

She did it for her convenience and to avoid a difficult situation.

She liked to chat but only to her friends.

∿ Well-Meaning

There were several of these creatures in a public place.

They were facing death.

She made a false assumption about the conditions necessary for their survival.

∿ Western Sunrise

No mirrors or reflections are involved. The man saw the celestial sun rise in front of him in the west.

He was on the planet Earth, not in a space rocket, or in space, or at the North or South Pole.

Looking west, the man first saw the sun set, then a little later he saw it slowly rise again.

∿ Westward Ho!

They walked only in an eastward direction. They never reached or passed through London.

The location of the restaurant is important.

∿ Window Pain

Both the windows are perfect squares.

Their areas are different.

They look different.

∿ Winning Numbers

If I participate, I will have the same chance as everyone else.

I am in no way prohibited from playing or winning.

The piece of paper has next week's winning lottery numbers on it. It also has last week's winning numbers.

∿ Wiped Out

She worked as a cleaner in a large building.

She cleaned on every floor.

She did much more work than was necessary.

∿ Without Drought

A technique was learned for increasing rainfall.

∿ The Woman in the Ditch

She was an actress.

She wanted to appear shorter than she really was.

∿ Wonder Horse

The horse did not deserve to win.

The weather was relevant.

This horse did not work as hard as the other horses in the race.

∾ **The Writer**

It was a long process.

Somebody helped him.

He used a part of his body that was not paralyzed.

∾ **The Wrong Ball**

The ball was clearly visible and accessible.

He did not touch the ball or examine it. He knew it wasn't his immediately upon seeing it.

∾ **You Can't Be Too Careful**

The pure medicine tastes very bitter.

They do not buy it as a medicine, although it is medicine.

It is effective against malaria.

SOLUTIONS

The Accident (page 119)

The other car was a hearse, and the passenger was already dead.

Acidic Action (page 59)

The woman's body was completely dissolved, but she had a plastic tooth that was not soluble in the acid.

Across the River (page 114)

They walked across; the river was frozen.

Adolf Hitler (page 17)

This apparently true incident took place during the First World War when Adolf Hitler was a private in the German army. He was wounded and the British soldier thought it would be unchivalrous to kill him.

Adrift in the Ocean (page 81)

They are in the vicinity of the mouth of the Amazon River. The outflow of river water is so huge that the Atlantic Ocean in that region consists of fresh water for hundreds of miles.

After-Shave (page 139)

The man was a bee-keeper. The after-shave changed his smell and the swarm of bees that knew him well now attacked him as a stranger.

Ageless (page 118)

The couple had been rock climbing together and they fell. He was rescued, but her body was trapped in a glacier. He was present when her body was finally recovered fifty years later.

Alex Ferguson (page 61)
Alex Ferguson chews gum incessantly during soccer games. The sale and use of chewing gum are illegal in Singapore.

Alone in a Boat (page 10)
The two animals were skunks that had been ejected from Noah's Ark because of the stench they were causing.

Ancient Antics (page 94)
No new species of animal has been domesticated in the last four thousand years. The ancients domesticated dogs, cats, cows, sheep, horses, etc.

Angry Response (page 10)
The man had said he would be home at 8:00 P.M. He arrived the following morning at 8:02 A.M.

Another Shooting (page 111)
In this true case, a robber had taken a woman as a hostage after his robbery. When the police tried to free her there was a shoot-out. The hostage was found to have been shot by a police bullet. The court decided that the robber had been guilty of her murder.

Anywhere in the World (page 67)
The pilot was due to fly from one point to another lying exactly opposite on the surface of the Earth. If we consider the Earth to be a sphere, then there are an infinite number of routes from a point A to a point B diametrically opposite to it. The pilot could set off in any direction and still have the same flight time. It follows that it would be possible to plan a straight course

from A to B which would pass over the place where the other man wanted to go.

The Archaeologist (page 52)

The ancient item was a dinosaur bone. When the professor's dog found the bone he took it out through the cat-flap and buried it in the garden!

The Archduke (page 137)

Archduke Ferdinand's uniform was sewn onto him so that he looked immaculately smart. It could not be removed quickly. His desire for a perfect appearance probably cost him his life.

Assault and Battery (page 16)

John is a newborn baby. The doctor slaps him to make him cry and use his lungs.

The Auction (page 78)

The man was bidding for a parrot that was such a good mimic that it bid against him!

Axe Attack (page 122)

This incident occurred during the French Revolution. The woman had seen her father beheaded at a public execution by a masked executioner wielding a large axe. The man kept the axe in his bathroom (he had to keep it somewhere!). When she saw the axe, the woman knew that the man must have been the executioner who had killed her father.

The Bad Driver (page 107)
James never drove his car during this period.

Bald Facts (page 87)
The woman was French and fell in love with a German officer during the German occupation of France. After the liberation, a mob shaved off all her hair and branded her a collaborator.

Bare Bones (page 76)
The student was pregnant. She had two femurs of her own, two of her unborn baby, and one in her hands.

Barren Patch (page 83)
Years earlier a troubled airplane had dumped its fuel onto this patch of land.

Beautiful Girls (page 33)
He had the two beautiful girls tattooed on his arms.

Below Par (page 28)
It was a nine-hole golf course.

The Big Room (page 138)
The large room is the ballroom of the Titanic. The barman went back to get a bottle of brandy for the lifeboat, but he never made it.

Biography (page 92)
The author wrote the biography of Marie Curie, the great French scientist who made many important discoveries concerning radioactivity. She won two Nobel prizes but died of leukemia

caused by radiation. The biographer collected many of her writings, belongings, and experimental apparatuses to help him write about her. Unfortunately, most of the memorabilia were highly contaminated with radioactivity, and he died later as a result of being exposed to it.

Bombs Away (page 64)

The plane was already in free fall.

The Book (page 71)

The man was the author of the book. On a visit to Tokyo, he recognized the cover design and was delighted to see that it had been translated into Japanese. He was more than happy to buy the book to show to his friends.

The Bookmark (page 33)

The man argues that he can use the dollar bill itself as a bookmark, and then spend it whenever he likes.

The Boss (page 100)

He fired the new employee on the spot!

Bostonian (page 28)

He was born in Boston, Massachusetts, in the early eighteenth century when it was still a British colony. He was British.

Bottled Up (page 61)

She took home the man's empty champagne bottles after a party. She then left them out with her garbage for collection in order to impress her neighbors.

Bouncing Baby (page 25)

The baby fell out of a first-floor window.

The Breeze (page 118)

The man was windsurfing from Cuba to the United States in a desperate attempt to reach freedom.

Brunelleschi's Challenge (page 114)

Brunelleschi brought the egg firmly down onto the table, thereby cracking and slightly flattening one end. The egg then stood on end. All the other contestants had assumed that the egg must remain unbroken, but this was never a condition.

Brush-off (page 50)

Amanda hangs up while she herself is speaking. She can subsequently claim they were disconnected.

The Building (page 115)

It was in medieval times and the man was on the run from a group of angry traders whom he had robbed. He reached a church and claimed sanctuary within it. His pursuers could not arrest him in the church and, if he waited long enough, he could get away.

The Burglary (page 109)

The couple had given their keys to an honest and conscientious neighbor. One day a delivery van had arrived. The van driver told the neighbor that he had a chest of drawers ordered by the couple for delivery. The neighbor unlocked the house and carefully watched the van driver and his mate carry the chest of drawers

SOLUTIONS

inside. An hour later, the van driver returned and apologized; he had delivered the chest to the wrong house. The neighbor again watched as the chest was removed. Hidden within this piece of furniture was a dwarf. He had, of course, removed all the small valuables he could find during his stay inside the house.

Burnt Wood (page 85)

Every two years England plays Australia at cricket for the "Ashes." Its name stems from an epitaph published in 1882 following Australia's first victory over England. The article lamented the death of English cricket and stated that its remains would be cremated. The following year the ashes of a burnt cricket stump were presented in an urn to the captain of the English team. The urn has remained ever since at Lord's Cricket Club in London. Each "Ashes" series consists of five or six five-day matches that are fiercely contested and generate a huge following in both countries.

Bus Stop I (page 125)

While repairing the chair, the man had accidentally stuck his hands to it with superglue. He was waiting for a bus to go to the hospital to have the chair removed from his hands.

Bus Stop II (page 126)

The road on which the building stands is on a steep hill. The woman prefers to go past the building and walk down the hill, rather than get out earlier and walk up the hill.

Business Rivalry (page 97)

Cain and Abel were rival train operators involved in the shipping of cattle by rail. When Abel lowered his shipping rates well below cost, Cain dropped out of the rail business and instead bought all the cattle he could find, making a fortune by shipping them to the market on Abel's trains.

By the River (page 36)

The man was about to start a boat race by firing a starting pistol.

Bypass (page 27)

When the bypass was built, a bridge was built over it so that townspeople living nearby, but on the other side of the bypass, could still easily reach the town market. Unfortunately, the bridge over the bypass was not high enough to allow the passage of trucks underneath, so their drivers had to continue using the road through the town.

Call Box (page 38)

She told the telephone company that people were making free international telephone calls because of a fault in the phone booth. They promptly sent an engineer to fix it.

Capsize (page 141)

The riverboat was crowded with passengers and was motoring down a tropical river when a large snake fell off an overhanging branch onto the boat. All the passengers rushed to the other side of the boat to get away from the snake. This unbalanced the boat, which capsized.

Car in the River (page 37)

The water in the river came up to the man's chest.

The Carpet Seller (page 94)

The cut is made, in feet, as shown here.

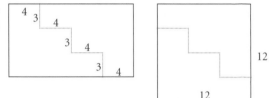

Cartoon Character (page 93)

The cartoon character who owes his existence to a misprint in a scientific journal is Popeye. He was invented to encourage children to eat spinach, which was thought to contain large amounts of iron. But this information was based on an error in a scientific journal—the decimal point had been put in the wrong place, making the iron content of spinach appear ten times higher than it actually was.

The Cartoonist (page 101)

He draws cartoons in which small objects are concealed. The drawings are used to test the ability of trainee pilots to detect targets in camouflaged backgrounds.

Cash in Hand (page 66)

Smith and Jones were travelling on the subway when a gang of muggers came into the car and started to take everyone's money. Smith offered to repay his debt to Jones just before the robbers reached them.

Catching a Bullet (page 134)

The first man fires the bullet vertically. The second man is standing at the top of a cliff. The bullet just reaches the top of its flight near the top of the cliff and it falls gently into the man's outstretched hand.

The problem can be restated so that the bullet is fired horizontally, in which case the solution is as follows:

A man fires a bullet from the back of a jet plane which is flying horizontally at the exact speed of the bullet and in the opposite direction to that of the bullet. Relative to the ground the bullet has no horizontal velocity. It would fall into the hand of a man standing under the plane at the point where the bullet was fired.

Chimney Problem (page 58)

The man on the tall chimney had a penknife in his pocket. With this he pried loose a brick from the top layer. He used the brick as a hammer. In this way, he gradually demolished the chimney by knocking out all the bricks and lowered himself to the ground.

The Cicada (page 129)

It is believed that the 17-year life cycle gives an advantage because 17 is a prime number. Consequently, it is most unlikely that any predator would have a life cycle in synchronization with this cicada. If there were a large population of cicada one year and a consequent increase in predators, then the cicada offspring generation, which would emerge in 17 years, would not coincide with a large generation of predators because their life cycles would not be factors of 17.

The Circle and the Line (page 144)

They were travelling in a hot-air balloon. When the circular circumference of the balloon crossed an electric power line, the balloon crashed and its passengers were killed.

The Circular Table (page 44)

She cuts out a piece of paper exactly the size of the table. She folds the paper in half twice, along any two diameters (by easily matching opposite sides of the circle). Where the two folds meet is the center. She then places the paper on top of the table.

Circular Tour (page 22)

Most people take one stride that is ever so slightly longer than their other stride. Over a period, this results in their walking in a huge circle. Incidentally, most athletes have a right stride longer than their left stride, relating to the fact that they always run clockwise around athletic tracks.

Clean Shaven (page 16)

Bearded men could be grabbed by the beard in close combat.

The Climber (page 102)

He hid one boot behind a rock and then hid the other a short distance farther on. He reasoned that, whereas one boot may be found, it was unlikely that the same person would find both boots, and since one boot would be of little or no value it would not be taken.

The Clinch (page 30)

Their teeth braces were locked.

The Cloth (page 143)
The man who died was shot in a duel. The man who waved the cloth gave the signal that the two duellists could commence.

The Code (page 49)
The correct answer to "Ten" is "Three." The code is the number of letters in the first word.

Complete Garbage (page 11)
The man was sleeping in a garbage can that was taken to the compactor.

Confectionery Manufacturer (page 32)
The workers are bees in a beehive.

The Container (page 54)
A ring.

The Courtier (page 117)
King Alfonso XIII of Spain was completely tone deaf. The man's function was to tell the king when the national anthem was being played, so that he could stand up.

Cowardly Act (page 129)
During World War I, some soldiers in the trenches deliberately exposed their hands or feet during heavy gunfire in the hope of sustaining an injury that would gain them a discharge and so avoid the risk of death.

The Crash (page 42)

One of the two trucks was a car transporter carrying six brand-new cars.

Creepy Crawlies (page 133)

He asks the managers of his local cinema, bars and community halls for the old cigarette ends, or butts, collected from containers. This debris they gladly give him in abundance, and he boils and strains the material to form a lethal nicotine-based insecticide which he uses to kill all the pests in his garden.

Cross the Gorge (page 112)

Very light fibers were sent across the gorge attached to a kite. These fibers were then used to pull strings across, which were used to pull ropes across, and so on until heavy cables were stretched across the gorge.

The Cruel King (page 121)

The king had asked the men to design and build the world's strongest strongroom, where he could safely keep his treasures. Once he was fully satisfied with the workings of the strongroom, he had the men executed so that they could tell no one its secrets.

Dali's Brother (page 72)

Salvador Dali died at age 7. Nine months later his brother was born and was also named Salvador. It was the younger Salvador Dali who became the famous surrealist painter.

Dance Ban (page 24)

The dance contest is a limbo dancing competition. The man banned was a dwarf, who had a natural advantage in getting under the low bars.

A Day at the Races (page 97)

The man was a thief who had made money at the races by picking pockets. After the policeman took down all his details, the man picked the policeman's pocket. The policeman returned to the station with no written record. He didn't remember the details because he didn't think he would need to remember them.

Dead Drunk (page 137)

He was at a deserted underground railway station. He urinated onto the electrified third rail, making a circuit to earth, and was electrocuted.

Dead Man, Dead Dog (page 122)

The field was next to a lake. The man had been poaching fish by dynamiting them. He threw a stick of dynamite into the lake. Unfortunately, the dog chased the stick, retrieved it, and carried it to the man, who had run away across the field—but to no avail.

The Deadly Climb (page 122)

The man who died had been scuba diving in the sea that morning. Ascending to the high altitude so soon gave him an attack of the "bends," where nitrogen dissolved in the bloodstream decompresses and is released as bubbles. It was this that killed him.

The Deadly Diamonds (page 53)
The thief simply took the box, turned it upside down, tilted it, and slid open the lid. The diamonds rolled out.

The Deadly Melody (page 136)
The woman was alone and asleep in her house in the middle of the night when she was awakened by the sound of her musical jewel box. She knew that a burglar was in her bedroom. She reached under her pillow, pulled out a gun and shot him.

Debugging (page 86)
If ants gathered around the place where a person had urinated, it was a strong indication that the person had diabetes. The ants were attracted by the sugar in the urine.

Depressurization (page 51)
The rattle he heard was a rattlesnake that had somehow got into the plane. By depressurizing the plane, he starved the snake of oxygen and it died. He was wearing an oxygen mask and survived.

Desert (page 52)
It was a very cold desert. He survived by eating snow or ice.

Doctor's Appointment (page 135)
The woman explained that she was the telephone repair engineer and had come to fix the phone. The new doctor had been lying about making the calls.

SOLUTIONS

Dogs Home (page 41)

He could only see half of the sign on the back of the truck because one door was open and the other closed. The full sign read Dogson's Home Produce. It was a delicatessen's van.

Don't Get Up (page 61)

The woman lives in an apartment building. She hears the phone ringing in the adjacent apartment. She knows that her neighbor, who is a brain surgeon, is out.

A Door Too Large (page 22)

This one is really a "snip"! The piece he cut off was too small, so he cut another piece off. The "it was too small" refers to the piece he had cut off, not the door.

The Drive (page 26)

The man was just learning to drive. He did not yet have a license, which would have allowed him to drive on the road, but he could do so on their private drive. The woman, his mother, turned the car around at the road so that he could continue to practice by driving back along their long drive.

Dud Car (page 30)

Nova means "won't go" in Spanish.

88 Too Big (page 77)

The man was an English tourist in the U.S. He was alone in an apartment when he had a heart attack. He crawled to the phone and dialed the English emergency number, 999, instead of the 911 used in America.

Elevator (page 41)

The woman was from out of town and had heard stories of violence and muggings in the big city. She found herself alone in an elevator with a large, fearsome-looking man who had a big Alsatian dog. The man said, "Sit, Lady!"

The terrified woman sat down only to see the dog do the same. The man cheerfully helped her up and they had a laugh about the incident.

The End of the War (page 113)

It is recorded that the war ended on a day when there was a total eclipse of the sun. Each of the armies took the eclipse as a sign that the gods were angry with them. Astronomers can date the eclipse very accurately.

The Engineer (page 104)

The engineer was killed when a large tree fell on him. The dam the engineer went to see had been built by beavers, and a particularly industrious one felled the tree.

Exceptional Gratitude (page 72)

Bill and Ted were neighbors. Ted kept chickens. Ted's chickens had been wandering through a gap in his fence and pecking around in Bill's garden. They had never laid an egg there. But after Bill thanked Ted for the eggs that his chickens had laid, Ted quickly fixed the fence to stop the chickens from getting out.

Export Drive (page 64)

Many Japanese exporters relocated their factories to a little Japanese town called Usa. They could honestly stamp on their products MADE IN USA.

Fair Deal (page 144)

The police arrested the dealer and charged her with murder.

Fair Fight (page 17)

The boxer was a dog that had just won the championship at a dog show.

The Fall (page 34)

He was on a roller coaster.

Fall of the Hall (page 129)

The building was owned by the National Geological Society, although it had not been originally designed for them. Over the years, the society's collection of rock specimens grew and eventually the weight of the rocks caused the building to collapse.

Fall of the Wall (page 40)

The guards were bribed.

The Farmer (page 102)

When the farmer awoke that morning he had seen a rainbow in the sky. It seemed to end in his field. He dug up the field in order to find the pot of gold!

Fill Her Up! (page 87)

The woman saved carefully and bought her husband the car as a surprise anniversary present. She had it delivered into their driveway and completed the paperwork with the salesman who brought it. Her husband was a cement truck driver. He was jealous and suspicious. He came home unexpectedly, and when he saw the new car in his driveway and his wife talking to a smartly dressed stranger, he assumed the worst. He reversed his truck and dumped his truck's load into the car.

Fingerprint Evidence (page 86)

When Bundy's apartment was searched, none of his fingerprints were found. This fact was used by the prosecution as evidence of his compulsion to clean fingerprints in all situations—showing his guilt.

Fired for Joining Mensa (page 14)

Anne works for Mensa in the administration of admission tests. Under Mensa's constitution, no member can be an employee.

500 Times (page 25)

Hairs on the head. Florence is a brunette, and Washington is a bald man.

Flipping Pages (page 12)

I was photocopying the book.

The Forger (page 108)

He was red-green color-blind. The note was colored red. (He had problems with traffic lights as well as paper!)

The Forgery (page 113)
When the calendar was adjusted in England in 1752, eleven days were skipped. The date on this document was one of the eleven days that never existed!

40 Feet Ahead (page 44)
The man walked around the Earth. Since he was walking on the surface of a sphere, his head, which was 6 feet farther away from the center of the sphere than his feet, travelled 2 pi × 6 feet farther. (It can be argued that it is impossible to walk around the Earth, but this does not matter. Any walk of any distance on the surface of the Earth involves the same principle. A walk of 26,000 miles on the Earth's surface would mean that the man's head travelled about 40 feet farther than his feet.)

Free Lunch (page 92)
The man was a piano tuner who had come to tune the piano in the restaurant. He brought his own tuning fork. The restaurateur repaid the service with a free lunch.

Full Refund (page 97)
The couple had a little baby with them. They were allowed into the theater on the condition that they leave if the baby cried, with their money refunded. After about 20 minutes, they realized that the movie was terrible, so the mother pinched her baby to make it cry. They left with a refund.

Garbage Nosiness (page 59)

On our street we put the cans out on the curb for collection every Monday morning. I forgot to put the can out two weeks in a row. Looking in my neighbor's can was the easiest way to confirm that I had missed the collection.

Gas Attack (page 85)

The unfortunate man was August Jager who had served in the German army in World War I. He was sentenced to ten years' imprisonment in 1932 for treason. He had deserted in 1915 and been taken by the French just before the Germans launched the first-ever poison gas attack. The French asked him what his gas mask was and he told them. Ironically, it was only in 1930, when the French General Ferry wrote his memoirs, that it was revealed that Jager had told the French about the impending attack. The French ignored the information and took no evasive action. However, the German court found Jager guilty of treason in view of the fact that he had not thrown away his gas mask.

Gaze Away (page 54)

The man was the King of England. Until comparatively recently, it was considered very bad manners to look directly at the monarch. People were expected to look down or away, and never in the King's face.

Getting Away with Murder (page 75)

Many years earlier, the man's wife had faked her own murder and had run off with her lover. The man had been tried for her murder and convicted. He had served a twenty-year sentence. When released, he found her and shot her, but he could not be convicted of the same crime twice.

The Golden Vase (page 108)

The thief hid in a broom closet after closing time at the museum. He opened the closet door and threw a boomerang which broke the electronic field before returning to him. He quickly grabbed the boomerang and retired to the closet. The guards came running but found everything in order. When they went away, the thief repeated the feat. This happened several times. Eventually, the guards decided that the electronic system was malfunctioning and they switched it off. The thief then sneaked out and replaced the vase with a replica.

Golf Bag (page 12)

To deliberately ignite the paper bag would be to interfere with his lie and incur a penalty. So while he pondered the problem he smoked a cigarette. He discarded the cigarette onto the bag and it burned. No penalty was incurred.

The Golfer (page 100)

Jones was on the wrong green. Two different holes had greens that were fairly close. The two holes lay in a straight line. Jones hit his putt hard in the direction of the other green.

Good-bye, Mother (page 35)

The young woman was presented with the bill for the old lady's meal. The lady had assured the waiter, "My daughter will pay."

Grease (page 66)
The man's head had been stuck in a railing. A fireman rubbed grease on the captive's head to help free him.

Great Detection (page 105)
He had written the note on the back of an envelope that had his name and address on the front!

The Great Wall (page 19)
He was an astronaut standing on the moon—from where the Great Wall of China is visible.

A Hairy Story (page 34)
She shaved her head!

Happy Birthday (page 58)
The man went to the eye doctor to have an eye test. The doctor looked at his record and noticed that today was his birthday.

The Hasty Packer (page 137)
She was a sky diver who packed her parachute too quickly. It did not deploy correctly when she pulled the ripcord.

The Hasty Robber (page 48)
He was fleeing from the scene of the crime and failed to see a police officer with a radar gun. He was stopped for speeding and ultimately convicted of robbery.

Headline News (page 105)
The editor knew that this trial was the big story of the day, so he had two versions of the newspaper printed—one with the story

that Jones was found guilty, and one with Jones found innocent. He then simply distributed the correct version.

Heartless (page 137)
He was a mime artist giving a stage performance. When he had the heart attack, the audience thought it was all part of the act and no one came to help him until it was too late.

The Helicopter (page 37)
The helicopter was hovering just over the helicopter landing pad on an oil platform out at sea.

Hide-and-Seek (page 24)
Jackie had a sudden attack of the hiccups. These were so loud and regular that most of the children easily heard her. John, however, was deaf.

High Blood Pressure (page 19)
Gerald is a giraffe. The average blood pressure of a giraffe is three times that of a human being. This higher pressure is needed to pump the blood up that long neck!

Hole in One (page 21)
She got a hole in one—but on the wrong green! Driving off the first tee, she holed out on the adjacent, 18th, green.

Holy Orders (page 46)
A child had released a helium-filled balloon in the church. It was high out of reach but clearly visible. The priest was going to shoot it down with an air gun.

Homecoming (page 27)

In this true story, the executive had had shipped back to New York a thirty-foot sailing junk (Chinese boat) that he had bought while in Hong Kong.

Homing Spaniards (page 116)

Whenever possible, the Spanish explorers took with them a mare who had recently given birth to a foal. They left the foal at their base. The mare would invariably lead them back.

Hosing Down (page 88)

This incident occurred just before the start of the Monaco Grand Prix race, which is held in the streets of Monte Carlo. Part of the course runs through a tunnel. When it rains outside, the firemen hose down the road in the tunnel in order to make the surface wet. This improves consistency and safety.

Houdini's Challenge (page 115)

He offered to "make the challenge even more difficult" by being locked inside the safe. He had guessed correctly that the safe was far easier to unlock from the inside than from the outside.

How to Choose a Builder (page 47)

He asked each builder to nominate an alternate in case he could not take up the contract. He gave the contract to the builder most often nominated as backup.

The Impostor (page 114)

The authorities asked the woman to take a blood test, and she agreed. The real Anastasia was a hemophiliac, who would never have consented to a blood test.

Invaluable (page 42)

The man stole a lottery ticket. It turned out to be a winning ticket for a big prize. If it had been a small prize, he could have claimed it safely and anonymously at any lottery shop. To claim a large prize he would have to report to the authorities. He did not know where the ticket had been bought. If the original owner went to the police, then it was likely the man could be identified as a thief and sent to prison. So he threw the ticket away.

The Investigator (page 104)

The man had made a claim against his employers for an industrial injury that he claimed had damaged his back so severely that he could no longer bend down. The private investigator had been hired to gain evidence that this was not so. He took photographs of the man bending down to examine his flat tire.

Invisible (page 79)

The object is an airplane propeller, which rotates so fast that it cannot be seen.

Jam Doughnut (page 112)

President John F. Kennedy, on his visit to Berlin, tried to express solidarity with the people of the city by saying in German, "Ich bin ein Berliner." Unfortunately, he had been badly advised, since

SOLUTIONS

the phrase "ein berliner" in common German use did not mean an inhabitant of Berlin but a jam doughnut.

Job Description (page 83)

The two men were sitting by the window in the restaurant. As the woman passed, one of the men made sexist remarks to the other man, implying that the woman made her living by immoral means. She stormed into the restaurant and went up to them and said, "Actually, I am a lipreader."

Job Lot (page 42)

The bricks he had bought were designed for building a chimney. They were all slightly curved and consequently of no use to the builder.

Keys in the Car (page 48)

The man had already phoned his wife, who was 100 miles away, and persuaded her to drive to him with the spare set of keys. He does not want to have to explain to her that her journey was unnecessary, and face her wrath.

Kid Stuff (page 47)

The expert believes that some drivers mistake children for adults and subconsciously assume that, because the figures are small, the children are farther away than they actually are.

Large and Small (page 70)

The strong, fit, large people were oarsmen taking instructions from their coxes in preparation for a rowing regatta.

Leadfoot and Gumshoe (page 12)

The woman is the wife of the chief of police. In order to avoid any impression of favoritism she accepted the ticket and paid the fine.

The Less-Costly Capital (page 125)

The capital city in question is La Paz, Bolivia. It is the world's highest capital, lying between 10,700 and 13,200 feet (3300 and 4100 meters) above sea level. At this altitude there is less oxygen and fires do not light easily. La Paz has very little need of a fire service, and so saves money.

Library Lunacy (page 39)

The library was moving to new premises but had very little money for the move. By giving the borrowers extra time, it ensured that borrowers moved most of the books.

The Lifeboat (page 43)

It was a wooden lifeboat. The wood swelled after two days at sea and sealed its own leaks.

Light Saving (page 124)

The sockets were adapted so that bulbs with a left-hand screw were used. Unlike most other bulbs in sockets, they had to be twisted clockwise to be released. When would-be thieves tried to unscrew the bulbs, they were unwittingly tightening them.

The Lumberjacks (page 31)

Joe uses his breaks to sharpen his axe.

Machine Forge (page 79)

This true story concerns a confidence trickster. He sells the machine to a crook claiming it will generate perfect forgeries. He demonstrates the machine by feeding in green paper. But this green paper is actually genuine $100 bills covered in thick green coloring. The machine simply removes the green coloring.

Man in Tights (page 13)

The man was Superman. He was lying next to a block of kryptonite, the one thing that could knock him out.

Man Overboard (page 19)

He fell into the Dead Sea, which lies between Israel and Jordan. The water of the Dead Sea is so salty and dense that anyone in it floats very easily.

The Man Who Got Water (page 57)

This is a true story from Russia. The man had intended to wash his car, but when he returned he found that it had been stolen.

The Man Who Returned Too Soon (page 141)

His home was a houseboat on the sea. He put on his scuba gear and dived 200 feet. One should ascend from such a depth slowly in order to depressurize. He came up too quickly and suffered a severe attack of the "bends," from which he died.

The Man Who Shot Himself (page 123)

This is based on an actual case. The men were members of rival gangs. When they met, one pulled a knife and stabbed the other in the stomach, leaving him to die slowly and in agony. The dying

SOLUTIONS   251

man shot himself to curtail the pain. The prosecution proved that the man would have died soon after from his stab wounds. The court found the man who had carried out the knife attack guilty of murder.

Matchless (page 124)
He was the first child born in Antarctica, and therefore the only person who is known to be the "first born on a continent."

Mickey Mouse's Girlfriend (page 130)
During the Battle of the Bulge in World War II, German soldiers speaking very good English and wearing American uniforms infiltrated the American forces to confuse and misdirect them. This question was designed to identify the impostors.

The Millionaire (page 101)
The man was Walt Disney. A mouse came to nibble the sandwiches and it behaved so comically that Walt put out some food for him every night. The mouse inspired the idea of Mickey Mouse, hence the Disney empire.

The Missing Diamond (page 132)
The thief had left a tape recorder in the room which had recorded the sound of the man opening and closing the safe. From the number of clicks the thief was able to work out the combination. (He could not tell whether to go left or right initially with the dial, so he tried each option in turn.)

Missing Items (page 55)

The ten-year-old boy has kneecaps, which babies do not have. These develop between the ages of two and five.

The Missing Money (page 24)

The man had on a different pair of trousers in which he just happened to leave five dollars.

Misunderstood (page 63)

The instructions given to police dogs are normally in a language not often spoken in the U.S., such as Hungarian or Czech. This is to make it unlikely that any person other than the trained police officers will be able to control the dog.

Motion Not Passed (page 13)

Although 35% of the people voted for the referendum motion and 14% against, there were not enough votes overall for a quorum to be reached. It needed 50% of the population to vote in order for the results to be valid. If another 1% had voted against the motion, it would have carried.

Motionless (page 115)

The man was having his portrait taken in the very first days of photography.

Murder (page 110)

The elderly woman was poisoned by her greedy nephew, who wanted to inherit her fortune. He sent her what looked like a mailer with a fantastic offer for a collector plate which he knew she would want to have. To order the plate, the offer had to be completed, folded and sealed, and sent back without delay. The nephew had put a slow-acting poison on the seal of the mailer. Once his aunt had licked the seal and posted the mailer, there was nothing to connect him to her murder.

Murder in the Newspaper (page 141)

The old man was a priest and he was sitting alone when he read the newspaper. That day a man had confessed to him that he had murdered his aunt for her money. The priest realized that the woman in the newspaper was the murder victim. The seal of the confessional meant that he could not report the incident to the police.

Mutilation (page 51)

He had committed a murder. His fingerprints had been found at the scene of the crime but his identity was not yet known to the police. He dipped the ends of his fingers in acid to destroy his fingerprints.

A Mysterious Death (page 120)

The unfortunate man had been hit by a tiny meteor that had penetrated his brain.

New Shoes (page 136)

She was a knife-thrower's assistant in a circus act. He was blindfolded and threw knives at her with unerring accuracy. Unfortunately her new shoes had much higher heels than her normal shoes. Therefore, she died.

No More Bore (page 82)

Winston Churchill told his butler to go to the door smoking one of Churchill's finest cigars.

No Response (page 95)

The man had a stutter. The stranger who asked him the question also had a stutter. The man thought that if he answered and stuttered, then the stranger would think that he was being mocked, so the man decided not to answer.

The Nonchalant Police Officer (page 45)

The police officer saw the incident on a TV screen in the window of a consumer electronics store. It was his favorite police-drama program!

The Nonchalant Wife (page 120)

The woman's husband had committed suicide three years earlier. The cat had knocked over the urn containing his ashes. After she finished her cup of coffee, she swept his remains back into the urn.

Nonconventional (page 90)

If a nun wants the salt, she asks the nun nearest the salt if she would like the mustard, which is near the first nun. The second nun would reply, "No, but do you want the salt?"

Nonexistent Actors (page 79)

The movie is *Sleuth*, starring Laurence Olivier and Michael Caine only. If moviegoers were not fooled into thinking that there were other actors involved, it would give the plot away. At one stage Caine leaves and returns in disguise.

The Nosy Student (page 68)
Judy hid her letters in her roommate's textbooks, as she knew that was the one place that the roommate would never look.

Noteworthy (page 57)
A burglar had broken into the woman's house and taken all her savings. In trying to collect the last bill that was stuffed into a jar, he tore it in half. She reported the incident to the police, and then took the half of the bill to her bank. They told her that a man had been in that morning with the matching half!

November 11 (page 59)
When data entry clerks entered customer records onto the computer, the date field had to be completed. However, they often did not have that data, so they simply keyed in 11/11/11.

Nun-plussed (page 32)
The nun was suffering from severe hiccups. The doctor examined her and told her she was pregnant. The shock cured her hiccups, but she ran out before he could explain that his "diagnosis" was only a ruse to rid her of the hiccups.

An Odd Number (page 124)
In the number 8549176320, the digits are arranged in alphabetical order.

Once Too Often (page 55)

Voting twice in the same election is electoral fraud—a serious offense.

One Inch Shorter (page 127)

He was an Air Force jet pilot who had had to eject after a midair collision. The ejector seat threw him out with an enormous acceleration of over one hundred Gs. This acceleration compressed the vertebrae in his back, making him an inch shorter. After medical treatment and rest, he recovered to his normal height.

One Mile (page 73)

When it was originally surveyed, two teams were sent out down the west side of South Dakota. One started from the north and one from the south. They missed! It was easier to put the kink in the border than to redo the survey.

Orange Trick (page 33)

Put it under the table.

Paddle Your Own Canoe (page 132)

This incident took place in Australia, where, at a certain time of year, the rains create a river that flows down a course and then eventually dries up. Effectively, the river is a body of water that moves from one point to another, then disappears.

Page 78 (page 71)

The woman was borrowing books for her disabled husband who was confined to the house and a voracious reader. She could not remember which books he had already read, so they had a scheme. Whenever he read a book, or if she brought back a book he did not like, he made a small pencil mark at the bottom of page 78. She could then tell which books to avoid.

The Painter (page 32)
He had painted the walls at the art galleries.

The Painting (page 131)
She said that this was the room where she meditated while standing on her head and that she had hung it upside down so she could view it as she meditated.

The Parcel (page 131)
The parcel contained her husband's sandwiches, which he had forgotten to take to work. He worked in the lost property office of the bus company.

Pass Protection (page 96)
I am describing the end of my journey. My destination is a subway station that is a starting point for many commuters. I bought and used a token at the start of my trip. I simply exit through the turnstiles, passing the lines of commuters coming in.

Pentagon Panic (page 70)
The missiles are thrown up out of the Earth's atmosphere and then plunge back to Earth. The Earth's rotation, therefore, affects their flight times. Since the Earth rotates from west to east, it follows that a missile will have a shorter flight time from Moscow to New York than vice versa.

Pentagon Puzzle (page 86)

The Pentagon was built in the 1940s, when the state of Virginia had strict segregation laws requiring that blacks and whites use different bathrooms.

The Perfect Murder (page 142)

Edward placed a tray on the edge of the kitchen table. He put some pans on one side of the tray and ice cubes on the other side. When eventually the ice melted, the weight of the pans caused the tray to fall off the table. The pans bounced on the floor and the alarm was activated. To the police, the tray, pans, and water looked to be part of the general disturbance in the kitchen.

Picture Purchase (page 10)

The picture was worthless, but it was in a fine frame that he intended to reuse.

The Pilot's Son (page 21)

The pilot was the boy's mother.

Point-Blank Shot (page 107)

This true story concerns a striptease dancer who was shot by a jilted boyfriend. Although naked, she was saved by a silicone breast implant that stopped the bullet.

Poisoned (page 108)

The poison had been put on his false teeth.

Police Visit (page 70)

The Japanese police first verify that you have a garage or parking space and then give you a permit to buy the car. Parking space is so scarce in Tokyo that, if you have no parking space, you are not allowed to own a car.

Poor Delivery (page 21)

The U.S. company stated its required delivery dates in its usual date format, i.e., month/day/year. The European company read the dates as European date format, i.e., day/month/year. So, if the American company asked for a delivery on the 5th day of July 1995, shown as 7/5/95, the European company would deliver the 7/5/95 shipment on the 7th of May!

Poor Dogs (page 138)

During WWII, German soldiers trained dogs to carry explosive charges under tanks and then wait there until the charge exploded, destroying dog and tank. They then released the dogs near Russian tank positions. Unfortunately for the Germans, Russian tanks did not smell at all like the German tanks on which the dogs had been trained, so the dogs hunted around until they found German tanks to sit under. Consequently, they had to be shot and the whole sorry scheme abandoned.

Poor Equipment (page 68)

The expensive piece of equipment was a very good watch. The man went to the North Pole, where all the world's time zones meet. Although the minute hand would be correct, the hour hand could be set to any of the time zone hours. There is, in effect, no "correct time" at the North Pole!

Poor Impersonation (page 132)

The heiress had a mannerism whereby she leaned her head to the left as she spoke. The actress rehearsed her gestures in front of a mirror, so she leaned her head to the right.

Poor Investment (page 79)

The object is the black box flight recorder from a crashed jetliner.

The Postman (page 98)

The postman walked around the outside of the wall. The dog followed him, gradually winding its lead around the tree. The effective length of the lead was eventually reduced so much that the dog could no longer reach the path, so the postman delivered the mail.

The Power of Tourism (page 76)

The place is Niagara Falls, where the water can be diverted from the falls in order to power generators. If the beautiful view of the waterfall was not demanded by the tourists, then much of the water could be channeled through turbines to provide electricity, thus lowering the price.

Precognition (page 30)

The lady was a postal worker delivering a registered letter addressed to Mrs. Turner.

The Professors (page 98)

The equation was $9 \times 9 = 81$ but they were looking at it from different sides of the table. So to one professor it was correct, but to the other it read $18 = 6 \times 6$, and so was wrong.

Promotion (page 83)

John was promoted very publicly. He was immediately head-hunted by a rival firm, and lured away with a salary he could not resist. The original company wanted to fire him, but that would have been costly. They knew that their rivals were desperate to recruit one of their top people. This way, they got rid of him and saddled their rivals with a dud.

The Quatorzième (page 101)

He works in a major restaurant and, if called upon, it is his job to join a party of thirteen people in order to bring the number up to fourteen. Thirteen is considered a very unlucky number when dining in Paris.

Radio Broadcast (page 23)

The noise that deterred the mosquitoes was a frequency too high for the human ear to hear. It drove away mosquitoes, but also, unfortunately, cats and dogs. Listeners complained that their beloved pets fled when the broadcast sound came on.

Radio Death (page 139)

The man is a disc jockey who during his show put on a long piece of music and slipped out of the studio in order to kill his wife. He had timed the plan perfectly and would claim that he was on air throughout the evening as his alibi. After killing the woman, he drove hurriedly back and turned on the radio. He heard the music repeating as the record skipped. He knew that his cover was blown and he shot himself.

The Ransom Note (page 91)
The police were able to get a DNA trace from the saliva on the back of the stamp. This matched the suspect's DNA.

Rare Event (page 46)
The numbers of the year 1961 read the same if you turned it upside down. This will not happen again until 6009.

Recovery (page 20)
The truck had broken down because its brakes had completely failed. The truck driver drove back towing the recovery vehicle. When he needed to slow, he signalled with his hand and the recovery truck driver applied his brakes, thereby slowing both vehicles.

Red Light (page 32)
The teenagers were travelling on the road that crossed the road the police officer was on. They drove through a green light.

Reentry (page 16)
The Guinness Book of Records, after 19 years of publication, became the second-best-selling book of all time and therefore got into itself.

Regular Arguments (page 33)

They were acting in a play which involved a violent argument.

Rejected Shoes (page 56)

The man found that the synthetic shoes generated a buildup of static electricity when he wore them around his carpeted office. He constantly got electric shocks, so he rejected them and went back to his old leather shoes.

Replacing the Leaves (page 89)

The girl has a fatal disease. She overheard the doctor tell her mother that by the time all the leaves have fallen from the trees she will be dead.

A Riddle (page 22)

The answer lies in the use of plurals. He did not have eyes, he had one eye. He saw two plums on a tree. He took one and left one, so he did not take "plums" or leave "plums."

Riddle of the Sphinx (page 18)

The answer is man, who crawls on all fours as a child, walks on two legs as an adult, and uses a walking stick in old age.

Right Off (page 96)

In this true incident, the car had been struck and destroyed by a large meteorite that the man found lying next to the car. The meteorite was rare and it was bought by a museum for over one million dollars.

SOLUTIONS

Robbery (page 106)
They started to unload the television sets and carry them back into the warehouse. When the police arrived, the robbers told the police that they were making a late delivery, and they were believed!

The Rock (page 118)
The man was a deep-sea diver. The sharp rock punctured his suit.

The Runner (page 99)
In this true incident, the man had been let out of prison for the day in order to enter the marathon. After completing the race, he kept on running to avoid returning to prison.

Russian Racer (page 13)
The Russian newspaper reported (correctly) that the American car came in next to last while the Russian car came in second.

Sacrifice (page 138)
One of the three was a strict vegetarian. He agreed that he should naturally be the sacrifice.

The Salesman (page 102)
The house was remote. When the salesman went to plug in the vacuum cleaner, he found that there was no electricity supply in the house.

School Friend (page 29)
Joe's old school friend was a woman called Louise.

Scuba Do (page 62)

The man, who was nearsighted, was on a diving vacation. He had broken his glasses and wore the diving mask, which had prescription lenses, in order to see properly.

Secret Assignment (page 94)

Ulam went to the university library and examined the library records of all the books borrowed by his students over the previous month. Los Alamos was a common link to nearly all of them.

The Secretary (page 103)

She had taken the only key to the office mailbox. She posted it back, so it wound up in the locked mailbox!

Sell More Beer (page 30)

The management consultant noticed that the barman was giving short measure. He told the barman to fill the glasses up to the top!

The Service (page 71)

The man was a stamp collector. The regular postage charge for a letter was around thirty cents but, as a special promotion, the post office declared that all letters posted during a certain week need only carry a three-cent stamp. He continued to use the regular stamps on the letters he sent to relatives, friends, and to himself, during that week, knowing that the stamped envelopes would be rare and become valuable to collectors.

Seven Bells (page 16)

It was originally a mistake, but the shopkeeper found that so many people came into his shop to point out the error that it increased his business.

Shaking a Fist (page 83)

The man suffered from severe allergic reactions to certain foods. He had inadvertently eaten something that had caused him to have a fit while driving. He veered across the road and came to a stop. He was unable to speak, but waved his hand at the policeman. He was wearing a bracelet indicating his condition. The policeman was therefore able to call for appropriate medical help.

A Shooting (page 111)

Rob and Bill were actors playing out a scene for a television crime series. Unbeknownst to Rob, someone with a grudge against Bill had substituted real bullets for the blanks that should have been in Rob's gun.

Shooting a Dead Man (page 59)

This puzzle is based on an incident in the film *The Untouchables*. There had been a shootout at a house and the police had captured a gangster who was refusing to give them the information they wanted. Sean Connery went outside and propped up against the window the body of another gangster, who had died earlier. Pretending the man was alive, he threatened him and then shot him. The prisoner was then convinced that Connery would stop at nothing to get the information he wanted. The prisoner talked.

The Shoplifter (page 74)

The shoplifter is a woman who pretends to be pregnant. She has a whole range of false "bellies" under her coat. After nine months, she naturally has to stop.

The Sign (page 136)

The car was stationary. The man's wife was deaf and dumb. She used sign language to tell her husband that she was having an affair with another man and that she was leaving him.

The Signal (page 128)

John stood with a dog whistle in his mouth. He gave three low whistles to his pet dog, James, to signal him to come and sit. The frequency of a dog whistle is too high for the human ear to hear but is audible to a dog.

Six-Foot Drop (page 14)

He caught it just above the ground.

Slow Drive (page 57)

The man was moving. He was a beekeeper. In his car he had a queen bee. His swarm of bees was flying with the car to follow the queen bee.

The Slow-Car Race (page 25)

The driver who raced back had jumped into his opponent's car, thus ensuring that his car would arrive back last and he would win.

Small Furniture (page 65)

The furniture is put into show houses on new housing estates. The smaller furniture makes all the rooms look larger.

Smart Appearance (page 41)

The mortuary had prepared Victor well for his funeral.

The Sniper (page 144)

He pours away the water and fills the bottle with gasoline from the car. He stuffs the handkerchief into the top of the bottle to make a Molotov cocktail. He waits until the sniper approaches the car and then lights the handkerchief before hurling the bottle at his attacker.

A Solution of Paint (page 50)

Samuel Plimsoll initiated a movement which led the British in 1875, and subsequently other nations, to draw a line, the Plimsoll line, on the hull of every cargo ship showing the maximum depth to which the ship could be loaded. Prior to this, many ships had sunk because they were overloaded.

Space Shuttle (page 64)

The exhaust plume of the space shuttle effectively grounds the space shuttle for a considerable part of its initial flight. Therefore, the shuttle could be struck by lightning. A plane is not grounded, so does not conduct lightning.

Speeding (page 111)

The man sped out of one country and stopped just over the border in another. The first policeman, who had chased him, had no jurisdiction in the second country. The second policeman had jurisdiction but could not arrest or prosecute the man for the speeding offense because it had taken place in another country.

Speeding Ticket (page 38)

In the very early days of automobiles, the speed limit was 8 miles per hour.

Spraying the Grass (page 81)

This happened just prior to the 1996 Atlanta Olympics. The groundskeeper sprayed the grass with organic green paint in order to make it look greener for the television audiences.

Stand at the Back (page 68)

A passenger sitting near the front had smuggled a poisonous snake onto the plane and it had escaped.

The Statue (page 69)

Blocks of ice were placed on the pedestal so that the ropes on the bottom of the statue fitted between them. The ropes were then withdrawn. As the ice melted, the statue was lowered until it lay firmly on the base.

Statue of an Insect (page 15)

The insect is the boll weevil, which wreaked havoc with the local cotton crop. As a result, many of the farmers switched to growing peanuts—and became very rich when peanut prices rose.

Steer Clear of the Banks (page 36)

The man was disabled. He got out of his car and onto his wheelchair. He used the wheelchair to go up and down the main street.

The Stiff Gate (page 113)

The host was Thomas Edison, the famous inventor. He explained that everyone who opened his stiff gate pumped ten gallons of water into his rooftop tank!

The Stockbroker (page 100)

The stockbroker was trying to launch his own business. He bought a mailing list of 4000 wealthy people and sent half of them a prediction that IBM stock would rise the next week. He sent the other half a prediction that IBM would fall. A week later, he chose the 2000 names to whom he had given the correct forecast, and split them into two. Half received a forecast that Exxon would rise. The other 1000 received a forecast that Exxon would fall. Those who received the forecast that came true were again divided, and so on. After doing this six times, the broker was left with 62 people who had all received from him a sequence of six correct forecasts! They, naturally, thought that the stockbroker was a fantastically accurate predictor of market movements.

The stockbroker then called each of them in turn and asked them to move their entire portfolios to his control. They readily agreed, and he had the large portfolio base he needed.

Stolen Finger (page 138)

He had faked his own kidnapping and demanded a large ransom. He sent in someone else's finger with his ring on it to add force to the ransom demand.

Stop/Go (page 125)

The people are graduate psychology students conducting an experiment to measure the popularity of various foreign nationalities. In Paris, the students placed German, British, Italian, or Spanish number plates and ID stickers (D, GB, I, E) in turn on the cars. They then drove around, stopping at lights, and measured the length of time it took for French motorists to lean on their horns after the lights changed. They were testing a theory—the shorter the time, the more unpopular the nationality shown on the car!

Straight Ahead (page 13)

The straight sections were specified so that they could be used as aircraft landing strips in case of war or emergency.

Strange Reactions (page 52)

They worked as testers in a chemical testing factory. Joan was testing an onion substitute while John was testing laughing gas.

Strangulation (page 11)

The famous dancer was Isadora Duncan, who was strangled when the long scarf she was wearing caught in the wheel of her sports car.

Striking the Elephant (page 50)

The man is playing billiards (or snooker or pool) with balls made of ivory. By pocketing a ball with his cue, he wins the match.

Stringing Along (page 127)

The man was taking part in a kite-flying competition. He glued tiny pieces of glass to his kite strings so that they would cut the strings of competitors' kites. He won the competition, but was subsequently disqualified.

The Suitcase and the Box (page 131)

The man had just been released from prison. While there, he had caught and painstakingly trained a cockroach. It was kept in a little box and could do tricks. He went into a bar to celebrate his release and got the cockroach to do one of its tricks on the bar. He called to the bartender, "Hey, look at this." Whereupon the bartender killed it with a blow from his towel, saying, "That's the third one today!"

Suspense (page 66)

The man was travelling on the Chinese railway system where, for historical reasons, at a certain point the gauge of the rails changes from narrow to wide. Rail cars are lifted bodily twenty feet in the air before being deposited on a frame with wheels of wider track.

Sweet in Pocket (page 129)

In 1945, Percy Le Baron Spencer, an engineer at Raytheon who was working on radar equipment, noticed that a candy in his pocket had melted. He correctly deduced that this was caused by

SOLUTIONS

microwave radiation that had agitated the molecules in the sweet. Following this discovery, Raytheon designed and patented the world's first microwave oven.

Sweet Wheat (page 135)
Wheat pollinates by wind. The farmer is protecting his own future crops from contamination by inferior pollen from his neighbors' crops.

The Swimmer (page 101)
In this actual incident, the officials refused to recognize Sylvia Ester's achievement because she swam in the nude.

T-Shirts (page 45)
A law was introduced making the wearing of seat belts compulsory for car drivers and passengers. Many Italians tried to circumvent the law. They wore the T-shirts in order to give the false impression that they were wearing seat belts.

Talking to Herself (page 18)
The woman was eighty-seven. The language she was speaking was dying out and she was the last person to know it. The man was an academic who filmed her to record the language before it was lost forever. (This puzzle is based on the true story of Dr. David Dalby's filming the last woman to speak the African language of Bikya.)

Teenage Party (page 128)
The father kept his bottle of gin in the freezer, where gin remains liquid even to very low temperatures. The watered-down gin, however, had frozen into a solid block within the bottle.

The Test (page 14)
The final instruction in the test was to ignore all the previous questions. The teacher had repeatedly told the students to read over the entire exam before beginning. The test was given to see how well the pupils could follow instructions.

Third Place (page 131)
The man was Charlie Chaplin. While on holiday he entered a Charlie Chaplin look-alike competition but he was placed third!

Thirsty (page 143)
His home was his ocean-going yacht. He lost his way and his radio following a storm on an ocean voyage and eventually ran out of fresh water.

Three Notes (page 135)
The woman was a traffic warden who wrote out three parking tickets. The bank robber had parked a stolen car which he intended to dump after the robbery, so he threw the ticket away. The tourist was returning to Bolivia shortly, so he threw his ticket away. The priest was sad because he would have to pay his fine.

Three Spirals (page 90)
The woman was a spy. She received record albums in the mail. When they were intercepted, they were found to contain music.

However, one side had two separate spirals, one inside the other. The inner groove contained the secret information. She was caught when the authorities noticed that one side of the record lasted only half as long as the other.

Time of Arrival (page 50)
When he came in, the boy had removed his shoes and placed them on top of the morning paper.

Title Role (page 41)
She received the title role in the movie Rebecca. Rebecca does not appear anywhere in this movie.

Too Polite (page 122)
The Japanese office worker was in an elevator at work. The doors opened and he saw an important senior executive. He bowed low and his head was caught in the closing elevator doors.

The Tower (page 25)
The tower was the Leaning Tower of Pisa. The man jumped off on the upper side and landed safely on the floor below.

The Tree and the Axe (page 28)
She bought a Christmas tree. After Christmas, she put it in the garden and the next day she chopped it up.

The Trial (page 107)
While those in the courtroom watched the door and waited for the missing man to appear, the accused man was being video-taped. When the video was later played for the jury, they could see

that the defendant did not even glance towards the door—he knew that the missing man was dead and could not return.

The Truck Driver (page 143)

One of the wheels of the truck had worked loose and come off a little earlier. It had continued to roll along the road. As he stood by his truck, he was hit by the runaway wheel.

The Twelve (page 113)

Only twelve men have walked on the surface of the moon.

Twin Trouble (page 38)

Bob and Sam were born on the night that the clocks are set back for summer time. Bob was born at 1:45 A.M. Sam was born 30 minutes later. The clocks were set back one hour at 2 A.M., so Sam's official time of birth was 1:15 A.M.

Two Clocks (page 80)

The man was an avid chess player. His wife gave him a chess clock. This consists of two identical clocks in one housing. Each clock records the time taken by one player for his moves in a competitive chess game.

The Two Drivers (page 47)

This incident took place in Saudi Arabia in 1995. It is illegal for women to drive in Saudi Arabia. One driver was a man and the other a woman. The police officer arrested the woman, who was charged and convicted.

Two Jugs (page 38)
The jugs were full of frozen cubes of lemonade and milk. They stayed separate even when poured into the one large vat.

Two Men (page 120)
The man who died was executed in a Malaysian jail for drug smuggling. The other man was in a hospital in Hong Kong awaiting a kidney transplant. He had arranged to buy the kidneys of the executed man.

Two Suitcases (page 45)
The man is on his way to check or leave the baggage for storage. Now he only has to pay for one item.

The Typist (page 39)
Typing eleven words per minute is going quite fast, if the language is Chinese!

The Unbroken Arm (page 72)
The healthy young girl put a cast on her arm before going to take a French oral examination. She figured (correctly) that the examiner would ask her about her injury. She came to the exam prepared with answers about how she broke it.

Unclimbed (page 18)
The largest-known extinct volcano is Mons Olympus on Mars.

The Unhappy Patient (page 109)

The man had stolen some diamond rings and swallowed them just before his arrest. The police doctor X-rayed him. He was charged. Then they simply waited for the loot to be recovered.

Unknown Recognition (page 17)

He was the identical twin brother of someone I knew well. I had heard of him but had never met him before.

The Unlucky Bed (page 55)

Every Friday morning, a cleaning woman comes to the ward with a vacuum cleaner. The most convenient electrical socket is the one to which the patient's life support machine is connected. She unplugs this for a few minutes while she does her work. The noise of the vacuum cleaner covers the patient's dying gasps. The cleaner reconnects the machine and goes to the next ward. (Although this story was reported as factual in a South African newspaper, it is almost certainly an urban legend.)

The Unlucky Gambler (page 48)

The unlucky gambler had drawn a "ticket" bearing the number $6\frac{7}{8}$, i.e., the hat label with the size marked on it.

The Unsuccessful Robbery (page 109)

The gang had arrived at the bank shortly after another gang had robbed the bank.

Untying the Ropes (page 140)

When the President was shot he was rushed to the hospital in a serious condition. When he died, all the ropes on the flagpoles across the country were loosened, as the flags were flown at half-mast.

Up in the Air (page 16)
A dead centipede!

Vanishing Point (page 125)
The place was the North Pole. The point is marked on the ice pack over the Arctic Sea. The ice pack drifts, and from time to time the point has to be adjusted. When he returned, the man read that the point marking the North Pole was being relocated.

The Ventriloquist (page 100)
The great ventriloquist was really only an average ventriloquist with a clever partner. He started his act with a standard routine with one or two different dummies. Then he would reach into a large chest and pull out another "dummy," who was really a dwarf that dressed and acted like a dummy. The rapid and humorous dialogue of the two men fooled the audience into believing they were seeing a virtuoso performance in ventriloquism.

Walking Backward (page 96)
The man walked backward from the front door as he varnished the wooden floor. He left the front door open for ventilation. When someone rang the doorbell, he quickly ran around to the front of the house in order to stop the person from walking inside onto the wet varnish.

Waterless Rivers (page 14)
A map.

Weak Case (page 57)

The police charged the man with stealing coins from a vending machine. He was given bail of $400, which he paid for entirely in quarters.

Well Dressed (page 46)

If it was someone she wanted to invite in, she said she had just come in. If it was someone she did not want to invite in, then she said she was just about to go out.

Well-Meaning (page 60)

The animal rights activist went into a restaurant where there were live lobsters in a tank. She bought them all to liberate them, but freed them into fresh water, where they all died because they can live only in salt water.

Western Sunrise (page 128)

He was the pilot of the Concorde. It took off shortly after sunset and flew west. It, therefore, caught up with the sun and the pilot saw the sun rise in front of him—in the west.

Westward Ho! (page 44)

(West) Bristol ―― Reading ―― London (East)

The two men walked to the railway station in Reading and boarded the train for Bristol at its western end. They walked to the restaurant car in the center of the train and had a long lunch. They then carried on walking east along the train, which arrived in Bristol.

SOLUTIONS

Window Pain (page 85)

Initially the square window has sides of about 1.4 feet and an area of 2 square feet. It is as shown at the right. The second window has sides of 2 feet and an area of 4 square feet.

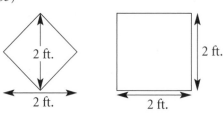

Winning Numbers (page 17)

One has to choose six numbers from sixty for the lotto jackpot. My piece of paper contains all sixty numbers, so it must contain the winning numbers.

Wiped Out (page 77)

The woman had been told to clean the elevators in a skyscraper. She had cleaned the same elevator on each floor!

Without Drought (page 112)

During the American Civil War it was noticed that the continued firing of cannons caused an increase in rainfall. From this it was learned that firing guns into clouds could cause them to release their water vapor in the form of rain.

The Woman in the Ditch (page 66)

She was the co-star in a movie and was playing opposite Alan Ladd, who, though a fine actor, was rather short. So as not to be seen towering over her co-star, the woman walked in a specially cut channel alongside Alan Ladd.

Wonder Horse (page 81)

In this true story, the race consisted of three laps. It was a very misty day. One of the horses stopped at the far side, of course, waited a lap for the other horses to come around, then rejoined the race and won. The jockey later confessed.

The Writer (page 58)

He winked one eye and thereby indicated to a very dedicated assistant each letter, word, and sentence of the book. He was Jean-Dominique Bauby, the French writer. The book he wrote by blinking, *The Diving Bell and the Butterfly*, was published just before his death in 1996 and became a bestseller.

The Wrong Ball (page 84)

It had been a cold night and the ball was lying in a small frozen puddle.

You Can't Be Too Careful (page 90)

The medicine is quinine, which is used to treat malaria and which people buy in tonic water. The British in India suffered badly from malaria until it was discovered that quinine cured and prevented it. Quinine tasted unpleasant, so they put it into carbonated water and created tonic water.

WALLY Test (page 145)

1. None.
2. It is best to take a photograph of a man with a camera.
3. All of them.

4. The window.

5. He drove in reverse.

6. Neither. The plane was over the Gulf of Mexico, so they both hit water.

7. Nine.

8. Most nuns use spoons.

9. To make the elevator move.

10. Lend me $13!

11. Time to get a new clock!

12. Two men, one of whom was a grandfather.

13. The archaeologist was right, of course. The coin had been found in a cloth which was carbon dated 200 B.C.

14. a) white; b) water (most people say milk).

Now rate your score on the following scale:

Number Right	Rating
12 to 14	WALLY Whiz
8 to 11	Smart Alec
4 to 7	WALLY
0 to 3	Ultra-WALLY

INDEX